PERFECTLY
AUTISTIC

Building Autism Bonds and
Creating Harmonious Connections

PERFECTLY AUTISTIC

...in every single way xxx

Written by Autistic Author

Emma Kendall

First published in 2019
by M and R Publishing
PO Box 2016
Andover
SP10 9JQ

contact@mandrpublishing.co.uk

www.emma-kendall.co.uk

Cover by M and R Publishing

ISBN 978-1-08153-409-7

Contents

Acknowledgements

Firstly, I would like to thank Chris, my university tutor, for always seeing my potential and making me feel validated.

I would also like to thank Andrea and all the autism associated lecturers at the University of Birmingham for all their hard work.

I am also very grateful to Lesley, my son's nursery teacher, for being my rock and supporting me through my son's assessment and diagnosis. I can't put into words how much I appreciate everything you did for him and me.

My heartfelt thanks go to Sian, my son's one-to-one support assistant at his school, for your dedicated support over the last two years. You will always be a huge part of his learning journey, and I am truly grateful for all your time and patience.

A huge thank you to my mum for always being there for me and being an amazing grandma to my two children.

My warmest appreciation must go to my grandma for being my best friend throughout my entire life, providing me with such happy memories.

Finally, thank you to my husband for supporting me through everything and being an amazing dad. You make our life complete; you are one in a million.

About the Author

Emma was diagnosed with Asperger's syndrome (AS)/high functioning autism (HFA) in her early thirties. She comes from a family that has many autism spectrum disorder (ASD) diagnosed members, including her 8-year-old son.

Emma has completed academic studies with the University of Birmingham (UK), specialising in Autism: Special Education (BPhil), where she graduated with a first-class degree.

Her educational background includes qualifications in Counselling, Communication and Personal Skills.
Emma's education and personal experiences with autism have provided a broad base to approach many topics.

She especially enjoys working with parents of autistic children.

Over the years, Emma has provided her services independently, helping families connect with and understand the complexities of the autism spectrum.

Books by Emma Kendall

Non-Fiction:

Perfectly Autistic: Post Diagnostic Support for Parents of
ASD Children

Autistic Christmas: How to Prepare for an Autism
Friendly Christmas

Helping You to Identify and Understand Autism
Masking: The Truth Behind the Mask

Fiction:

The Adele Fox Series:

Making Sense of Love

A Different Kind of Love

Memories Full of Love

Join my Facebook page:

Emma Kendall Author

To receive updates on future releases, bonus content and more, visit:

www.emma-kendall.co.uk

Glossary of Terms, Abbreviations and Acronyms

ADD	Attention deficit disorder
ADHD	Attention deficit hyperactivity disorder
ADI-R	The Autism Diagnostic Interview – Revised
ADOS	The Autism Diagnostic Observation Schedule
AD	Anxiety disorder
ASC	Autism spectrum condition
ASD	Autism spectrum disorder
AS	Asperger's syndrome
Aspie	A shortened name referring to someone with Asperger's syndrome
Autie	A shortened name referring to someone with autism.
BPD	Bipolar disorder
CAMHS	Child Adolescent Mental Health Services
DISCO	The Diagnostic Interview for Social and Communication Disorders
DSM-V	Diagnostic and Statistical Manual of Mental Disorders (5th Edition)

EarlyBird Programme	Three-month programme for parents of children that have received an ASD diagnosis and are under five years of age
Echolalia	Repetition of speech (copying and repeating another person's speech)
GP	General Practitioner
HFA	High functioning autism
ICD-10	International Classification of Diseases and Related Health Problems (10th Revision)
LFA	Low functioning autism
Mute	Refraining from speech
NAS	National Autistic Society
NHS	National Health Service
Non-verbal	Not involving or using words for speech
OCD	Obsessive compulsive disorder
PDA	Pathological demand avoidance
PIP	Personal Independence Payment
Pre-verbal	Words existing or occurring before speech develops
Social script	A written or spoken narrative used to improve the understanding of difficult to comprehend situations

Stimming	Used to describe self-stimulatory behaviour. Known as - repetitive behaviours such as hand flapping, rocking, spinning, clapping, humming, tapping
Stressor	Emotional response to the environment, or emotional stimulus
Trigger	Something that causes you to respond or react in a particular way

Introduction

An autism spectrum disorder (ASD) diagnosis can be life-changing, not just for your child but your family too. Whether you're an autism expert or merely learning the basics, there will always be something new to learn. Simply because autism spectrum disorders are highly complex and unique to each individual.

Studying autism was like a form of therapy for me. Not only was it a learning journey academically, but it also answered many questions regarding myself. The studies and research I took part in triggered deep personal acknowledgements of my own autistic characteristics and identity. I noticed the more I understood my autistic identity, the better I felt about myself. Which had a positive impact on my mental health and improved the way I function in general.

As an autistic adult in my late thirties, I've seen a huge shift in how society understands and recognises autism. We have gone from society knowing very little, thinking girls can't be autistic (autism was previously viewed as a boy's disorder) to now seeing girls, boys, teenagers, adults, mums, dads, grandparents, celebrities, you name it, being diagnosed. This awareness has increased drastically, and as a result, autism is now viewed and acknowledged as a broad-spectrum disorder. As this knowledge has increased, the criteria of what it means to receive an ASD diagnosis has also broadened. With this, it brings enormous confusion when trying to understand what it means to be autistic.

I didn't learn overnight what it meant for me to be autistic or what support I needed to function as a wife, a mum or just Emma. It has taken years to understand my sensory difficulties, my specific communication differences (the way I use language different to others), what triggers me, why my brain doesn't process certain information, and so on.

I often wonder how this must feel for parents trying to understand their autistic child. If I've struggled, then how on earth must other parents feel? Especially if they are learning everything from scratch.

Looking back to when I started the autism referral process with my son (he was two years old), there was very little support or information readily available. There were times when I felt lost and lonely and just needed to talk to somebody that could understand.

My journey has shown me there are many families out there just like mine who need guidance and support, and for that reason, I decided to put this book together with information that I hope can be of use to others.

There are so many aspects and variations to autism spectrum disorders, no single book can give you every answer specific to your child. Also, you may find my experiences to be slightly or completely different to yours, but that doesn't mean you can't learn anything from me.

If you can familiarise yourself with the basic approaches and autism knowledge, then it can hopefully provide you with the skills and information to help make parenting an autistic child that much easier.

I wrote this book to offer ASD information and experiences from an autistic perspective. I also include the strategies I find to be useful when understanding and connecting with an autistic child.

This book will be helpful for families that have a child that has recently received an ASD diagnosis. It will also be beneficial to families that are still learning how to support their child.

Or, if you just want to read about autism from a different perspective, then this book will provide that.

The context will reflect on important aspects such as autism terminology and how to discuss the diagnosis with your child, friends and family. How to help your child understand their diagnosis and how they can explain to others that they are autistic.

Also, how to connect with your child, helping them to thrive, and advocate their needs. How to use calming and coping strategies, recognise and address autistic behaviours, and help your child build confidence and self-esteem.

Throughout the book, I will use the term autistic spectrum disorder/ASD opposed to autistic spectrum condition/ASC. Simply because the term ASD is currently used in legislation, academic literature, and medical practices. It is also a universally recognised term.

I will also use the term autistic (as a collective term) when describing all children and adults diagnosed with ASD and associated disorders.

The age range I predominantly focus on is that of school-aged autistic children. I don't like to say a specific age range because, ultimately, autistic children are not necessarily typically developed according to the generic stereotypical mile stones and developmental trajectory. Because of this, I couldn't possibly pinpoint a specific age.

I focus on pre-verbal and verbal children in particular. However, some aspects will cover non-verbal children.

I hope to reduce common misunderstandings and worrisome matters and provide you with the foundations to understand how to connect with your child and create an autism bond.

Thank you for taking the time to read my book; I hope you enjoy it.

Chapter 1

Autism Spectrum Overview

Over the past few decades, the diagnosis of autism spectrum disorders (ASDs) in children and adults has increased tremendously. This has undoubtedly prompted the need for medical literature and legislation to be updated and adjusted to help diagnose and support the needs of autistic people. There has also been an increase in adult autistic advocates that are successfully helping to bring a deeper understanding to the challenges that are presented daily for the autistic population. Even though we are witnessing this positive progress, there is, undeniably, a significant number of people working with (or supporting) those on the autism spectrum that are having difficulties connecting to, and understanding, the characteristics and needs of autistic people.

Many reasons contribute to this. First, the way autism spectrum disorders have been assessed and diagnosed in the past has not ultimately come from a universal assessment.

There are many diagnostic assessments such as:

DISCO	The Diagnostic Interview for Social and Communication Disorders.
ADOS	The Autism Diagnostic Observation Schedule.
ADI-R	The Autism Diagnostic Interview - Revised.
Psychological Evaluation	Behavioural observation carried out by specially trained physicians, psychologists, speech therapists, etc.

The ASD assessments are carried out by many organisations such as the NHS (National Health Service), private autism charities, self-employed or private psychologists and private mental health/autism support teams. Even though the strategies that these organisations use are effective, they don't necessarily use the same assessment format. This has resulted in many methods being used to determine the diagnosis of ASD.

The diagnosis result can be determined by a score of meeting specific criteria and/or by being interviewed. It could be a score and/or assessor's discretion and professional opinion that determines whether an individual meets the criteria for ASD diagnosis or not.

There are no definitive tests, such as DNA/genetic testing, currently being used in the public domain to diagnose ASD. Therefore, it is the responsibility of the assessing clinicians to determine and provide a clinical opinion. We trust that the assessing clinicians have had adequate training and accept that their opinion is correct.

Over the years, I have encountered many adults and children who have been assessed and told they are not autistic, only to be assessed by another clinician and told they are definitely autistic. These discrepancies lead us to question the efficacy of how autism is identified, not just within society, but the professional sector also.

Autistic or not, the whole process of going through an autism assessment can be stressful and take a long time. I've heard many autistic adults and parents of autistic children say they are often made to feel like they need to prove their autistic characteristics to a GP (General Practitioner), teacher, support worker and so on, before they can even get a referral for an ASD assessment. Then, when they finally get an ASD diagnosis, there is very little support afterwards. Therefore, they are left to their own devices to learn and understand how to support somebody on the autism spectrum.

A few years ago, I had a parent approach me and ask if I'd go with them to the initial GP appointment to ask for a referral for ASD for their teenage child. I was happy to be of assistance and went with them. I was shocked to find the GP knew very little about ASD.

He initially sat for five minutes reading through the child's medical notes, then proceeded to ask questions such as, "Is your child simple?"

I couldn't believe what I was hearing; I was utterly horrified. It was then that I had to step in and intervene, explaining to the GP why, how and where he needed to refer the child to, because clearly, he hadn't done this before. The GP was rude to me afterwards, he wasn't happy that I had stepped in, but ultimately, if I had not been there, I realised that the child might not have even received a referral. Three months later, the child received a diagnosis of Asperger's syndrome (AS).

Not only do we find differences in the way autism is referred and diagnosed, but we also find many diagnostic terms such as high functioning autism, Asperger's syndrome, classic autism, and ASD Level 1, 2 or 3. The continuous changes have presented a lot of confusion for those trying to understand what it means exactly to receive an autistic diagnosis.

For example, below is a list of autism spectrum terms that have been used within the professional sector and society to identify autistic people and their associated characteristics.

General Autistic Terms	Associated Characteristics
Classic autism	Require daily supervision and/or support
Autistic disorder	for specific activities, e.g.,
Severe autism	washing/showering, feeding, getting
Kanner's autism	dressed and so on.
Low functioning autism	Typically develop spoken language later than their peers. May be intellectually
Profound autism	disabled such as non-verbal, pre-verbal,
Infantile autism	mute, communicating through
Childhood autism	signs/picture boards/electronic

Pervasive development disorder Global development disorder	tablet/apps. Present difficulties in social interaction and communication. Communicate via behaviours, e.g., aggression, frustration, screeching, etc. Exhibit challenging behaviours, for instance, demand avoidance (refuse or ignore requests), self-stimulatory behaviour (rocking, flapping hands, head-banging), use socially inappropriate behaviour (e.g., taking clothes off in public).
Regressive autism Little professor's syndrome Asperger's syndrome Geek syndrome Mild autism High functioning autism Pathological demand avoidance	Typically, no language delay. May develop spoken language/verbal skills but often present difficulties in social interaction and communication. Often have average or above-average intelligence/IQ, e.g., good remote memory for technical and factual information. Often have sensory challenges such as not being able to tolerate specific noises, smells or fabrics. Have repetitive stereotypical behaviours and/or a need for routine.
Autism spectrum disorder Autism spectrum condition ASD Levels 1, 2 or 3	These terms are used collectively to describe or group autistic associated subtypes and characteristics.

Many of the diagnostic terms and definitions used to identify autistic people are commonly referred to in society as labels or subtypes. These labels generally have many overlapping characteristics producing many similarities. Therefore, all these differing labels can be confusing when trying to understand the autism spectrum, which terms to use, and what they mean.

Autistic people also have their own personal preferences for terms or labels that are not necessarily used within the autism professional sector or amongst parents of autistic children. For example, referring to themselves as Aspie (abbreviation of Asperger's syndrome) or Autie (abbreviation of autism). They may refer to themselves as 'I'm on the autism spectrum.' Therefore, it has become common in recent years for autistic people to be asked, "So, where *on* the autism spectrum are you?"

Ultimately, there is no generic way to answer this. Autistic people may all share core characteristics, but they are incredibly individual in the way they present themselves. This is due to their differing areas of limitations and abilities, their personality, the support they receive, their environment, etc. There are many contributing factors that make autistic people different and individual.

Functioning labels (high or low functioning) can also be misconstrued within society and tend to cause a lot of controversy within the autistic population. To deem someone as high functioning or low functioning can be viewed as an inaccurate way of identifying their needs. This is because many autistic individuals can be both high and low functioning, depending on the circumstances. For example, an autistic child could function adequately at home, but put that child in a school environment their ability to function can be extremely hindered. This is because the circumstances have completely changed due to unavoidable social demands, changes of routine, unpredictability, and so forth.

In recent years Asperger's syndrome has commonly been replaced with the term high functioning autism (HFA), or sometimes they use both terms. For example, when I was assessed, they diagnosed me with Asperger's syndrome/high functioning autism. Even I questioned if I should refer to myself as Asperger's, autistic, or both? I hadn't realised back then that the labels the assessing team used were to be viewed as the same definition.

As I write this in 2019, autism diagnostic teams in the UK are still diagnosing Asperger's syndrome in certain practices, in accordance with the International Classification of Diseases and Related Health Problems, 10th Revision (ICD-10), unlike America, where they have removed the Asperger's syndrome diagnosis from their standard diagnostic manual, the Diagnostic and Statistical Manual of Mental Disorders, 5th Edition (DSM-V). American practices now refer to the terms ASD Levels 1, 2 or 3.

Level 1   Requiring support.

Level 2   Requiring substantial support.

Level 3   Requiring very substantial support.

In the UK, we mainly use the ICD-10 codes of practice, which will soon be updated to ICD-11. It has been suggested that the diagnosis of autism, Asperger's syndrome, and other associated developmental disorders will be collapsed into a single diagnosis of ASD, mirroring that of the DSM-V. Many diagnosticians are already shifting and using the collective terms ASD, ASC, or autistic/ASD.

It's clear that the changes are most definitely happening, and it is becoming more common to hear the abbreviated term ASD when referring to autistic people. Back when I was diagnosed, it was generally autism or Asperger's syndrome. This collective term ASD, is similarly being used like other disorder abbreviations such as Attention Deficit Hyperactivity Disorder (ADHD), Obsessive Compulsive Disorder (OCD), Bipolar Disorder (BPD) or Attention Deficit Disorder (ADD).

Most people recognise disorders like these being typically used within society in their abbreviated form. For example, you rarely hear people saying, 'my child has attention deficit hyperactivity disorder,' they just say, 'my child has ADHD.'

It is socially acceptable to use an abbreviated term when describing people as a specific diagnosed disorder. Just like it's becoming socially acceptable to refer to an autistic child as an ASD child. The changes in descriptive use of language are allowing medical literature to use the abbreviation ASD as an umbrella term when describing all neurodevelopmental disorders.

The use of autistic descriptive language can also be confusing for parents. For example, should we say, 'my friend is autistic' or 'my friend has autism?' This is known as identity-first or person-first language. Through experience, I have found that television shows, news channels and media outlets will generally use person-first language. For example, he has autism, or he suffers with autism. The autistic community tends to use identity-first language. For example, 'I'm autistic' or 'my autistic child.'

Similarly, there are also many views on whether we should use the term 'disorder' or 'condition.' There is no standard set term that is used within society. The choice to use disorder or condition differs due to personal preference and perspective, as it depends on how you view your child's or your own diagnosis, and autism in general.

A few years back, when I was at a university tutorial, I was asked, "Which term do you use to identify?" To which I light-heartedly replied, "I use disorder because I'm a very disordered person." But that's just how I feel about myself; I don't place great importance on my label(s) because at the end of the day, whatever I am diagnosed with, I'm still *me*, 'Emma.'

Personally, I don't think there is a right or wrong way when using descriptive language and disorder or condition. People will use the terms that they best identify with, which is totally fine and subjective to the individual. When my son is older, I will teach him to identify with the terms and language he feels most comfortable using.

There will undoubtedly be many varying opinions on how autistic people should identify themselves and discussions on which language should be used.

Studies such as, 'Which terms should be used to describe autism? Perspectives from the UK autism community, 2015,' are finding there is no specific preference. This shows we are teaching our children and adults to be themselves and embrace who they are, and that it is down to the personal choice of the individual. However, this does not mean there aren't people who prefer to use specific terms; this is where being mindful of other people's perspectives is important.

The diverse, complex terms can cause a lot of controversy amongst autistic people, parents of autistic children, and other members of society. This is because there are so many differing views of what it means to be autistic or have autism. For example:

- Some people don't like the way others use certain terms and phrases. They can be very passionate about only using their preferred terminology and expect others to comply. Like it's an *autism rule.*
- Parents may prefer to say, *'My child has autism.'* preferring to separate the diagnosis from the child. This can be viewed as not accepting that your child is intrinsically autistic.
- I find there are also many autistic people and parents who really don't care about how they are labelled or the terminology used and just like to

recognise that they are simply children. Not a diagnosis, label, or abbreviation.

Instead of demeaning all these differing views, maybe we should ask why people use their specific terms? Perhaps it's because that's what they have been taught and don't know that there are many terms that can be used.

Every situation is different and purely subjective to each individual. This is understandable and to be expected when referring to such a diverse disorder with so many varied characteristics. Therefore, it is important to allow others to make their own choices, and to not judge their circumstances or preferred terminology, just accept we are all different, therefore will have different opinions.

A particular phrase that raises divided opinion is when autistic people are referred to as '*suffering with autism*,' or '*suffering from autism*.' Some autistic people will find the term *suffering* to be very offensive. As an autistic person myself, I truly understand why they would feel that way. I also understand why some people use this terminology because there are lots of people who do actually suffer from being autistic. Again, it is all down to personal circumstances. Autistic people are all individual, and it is the choice of the autistic child (or adult) how they would like to be referred to.

When we combine all these autism intricacies together, i.e. differences in referrals, diagnostic teams, labels, terminology/use of language, and so on, it's easy to see why it can be overly confusing when trying to understand the complexities of autism.

As long as people are mindful of the terms they use and think of people's feelings when describing autistic children and adults, then we can find balance by respecting all perspectives.

Chapter 2

The Diagnosis

It is well known within the autism community that gaining a referral and diagnosis for your autistic child is not always easy. It can be emotionally draining and stressful, yet we plough through this because we know how important it is for our children to be recognised that they have specific needs that require specialised support—knowing that without a diagnosis, there is very little help out there.

An autism diagnosis is not only important to gain support but can be equally significant for many reasons; a diagnosis can incite self-awareness and can help children to understand their differences or their areas of limitation and abilities (weaknesses and strengths). A diagnosis also helps children to receive support in school, future employment and future relationships.

When autistic people are clinically diagnosed, they don't receive options for how they would like to be identified. The title of their clinical diagnosis is applied and given to them by the medical sector. It can be quite unnerving receiving a label you know nothing about; it is very important to ensure that you and your child understand why they are receiving a diagnosis and what it means specifically for them.

Before you decide if and when you would like to discuss the diagnosis with your child, I think it's essential to have time for yourself to reflect on how you are feeling about the situation.

Many parents will experience a rollercoaster of emotions, and this is completely normal. One minute you may feel ecstatic because your child can now obtain access to the support they require; the next minute, you may feel shocked and full of bewilderment. It can be surprising to find many parents expect the autism diagnosis, but don't prepare for the whole new level of worry and nervousness that comes with it.

After receiving an autism diagnosis, generally, you will find it is followed by a descriptive assessment report which lists and defines the characteristics of the child. Initially, the report can be highly overwhelming to read. You may come across lots of new terms and information that you don't understand. The descriptions of your child may seem somewhat daunting and negative, which can be difficult to comprehend.

I hear all too often from parents who, once they have received a diagnosis, were left to their own devices with no post-diagnostic support. The lack of support can significantly impact how parents deal with the outcome and how they approach their child regarding autism.

I have come across many parents who have found the whole process to be overwhelming, and find it difficult to accept their child is autistic. There can be many reasons for this such as, no post-diagnostic support from services, unsupportive family members, their own belief system of what autism is, the feeling of not wanting your child to be stigmatised with a label, not seeing that there are any issues, etc. This will ultimately be respective of the parents' own personal circumstances.

Let's not forget, autism spectrum disorders have only become recognised within the public domain in the past few decades, so the older generations will not have experienced autism like the younger generations today. If you are one of those people struggling with the whole process, then the fact that you are reading this book shows you care and want to learn. I hope I can help make things easier for you.

There are parents that are fine with their child being autistic but may not feel the need to inform them of their diagnosis, choosing to wait until difficulties arise. Some worry that their child may use being autistic as an excuse, fearing it could cause them to become lazy, uncooperative and regress in certain areas of development.

There are parents that may not be comfortable labelling them for school reasons, worrying that they may lose friends because of the associated stigma and people's perceptions, and this is simply the parents' way of protecting their child from being automatically judged.

Either way, whether you tell your child or not, that is your choice; every situation is different and comes down to personal circumstances.

There will be many parents that will need time to learn about autism and familiarise themselves with the autistic terms before they can even begin trying to discuss it with their child. It is a known fact that autistic people, and children especially, tend to be very inquisitive; therefore, it's important to get it right when explaining and describing what an autism diagnosis means for them.

You may be a parent of an autistic child who is completely oblivious to their autistic diagnosis and the whole assessment process; therefore, it'll not impact them at all. But for others, it will be life-changing, and many children will enter a phase of having an identity crisis. It is important to give your child time to reflect on how they feel (in their own way).

It is also important to recognise that your autistic child may express their emotions entirely different from that of a typically developing child. They may not know how to communicate their feelings, and you may see behavioural changes or withdrawal. This is completely normal, so be patient and, if possible, do not change how they cope with their diagnosis, as it may create additional issues. It is important to give them time to process everything and to not pressure them into accepting and understanding it straight away. It could take one week, one month, one year or even ten years or more to understand what it means for them to be autistic. This may be because not all autistic people see themselves as different and don't see the differences that a parent or a professional may see, and this is because how they live life is just normal and perfectly fine to them.

When sharing the outcome of an autism diagnosis with a child, it is important to know what the diagnostic term they have been given means. This may sound like an obvious thing to do, but it's surprising how many parents I hear saying, "My child has been diagnosed with Asperger's syndrome, does this mean he's autistic?" or "He's only just met the criteria for an ASD diagnosis, does this mean he has mild autism?"

It is very common to see parents, support workers, teachers, etc, not understanding the autistic terminology because of there being so many terms and subtypes of ASD. If you are unsure of the diagnosis, it would be beneficial to discuss any questions you may have with someone from the autism team who provided the assessment and report.

The adults who support the child, i.e. the parents, family, and teachers, are usually the ones that have to help the child learn and understand what it means to be autistic. Therefore, these people need to have some understanding of autism to be able to connect with the child so that they can explain to the child their specific needs.

After you have given yourself time to reflect and understand how to discuss everything, decide if it's the right time to discuss the diagnosis with your child and consider if they are mature enough to comprehend what they are being told.

If your child is at an age where they understand their involvement in the assessment process, inevitably, it will intrigue them to find out the results of the diagnostic decision. This means that you may not have sufficient time to process the diagnosis yourself before discussing it with your child, which can be puzzling and overwhelming.

Personally, I think the age range that is the most difficult to explain a diagnosis to is the teenage years. Teenagers tend to have stronger reactions and opinions than younger children. They may also have a lot more going on in life, such as puberty, transitioning to adulthood and social life.

Many parents of children who received a diagnosis before they moved to the secondary stage of education said they were glad because it helped the child understand their difficulties when transitioning to the new high school and environment. For example, when making new friends, trying to fit in, recognising why and where they are different (reduces peer pressure), enabling them to advocate their needs and reach out for support when required.

Over the years, when I have spoken with autistic adults regarding late diagnosis (diagnosed in adulthood), most have said they would have preferred to have been diagnosed and told of their autism spectrum disorder as early as possible. If they had known, they would have done things differently in life and not struggled so much, as they would have had a better understanding of their difficulties.

Hiding a diagnosis from an older child might anger them and cause issues later on, especially if your family has known about the diagnosis for a long time, and the child finds out indirectly from another person rather than you. Autistic people tend to see things in black and white and have a strong sense of right and wrong. Trying to hide things from them could possibly create a feeling of distrust.

Helping your child understand the diagnosis.

When discussing the diagnosis with your child, there is no set way of doing it. I think the main thing is to concentrate on explaining and communicating in a way that they can process and comprehend. Your delivery and description will impact how they receive the information. So, try to explain it in the most loving and considerate way that you can, and be positive. Autism is your child's normal, so normalising it from the beginning will prevent them from feeling alienated.

Try not to make them feel as though they are being singled out—like they don't fit in. The feeling of being alone and isolated could possibly make them shut off altogether and not want to discuss anything that will make them feel like an outsider.

Try to explain your child's differences with confidence, embracing their diagnostic label. Don't see autism as a word to be embarrassed about or shy away from. Instead, make them feel secure, encourage them to feel proud about who they are, and not care about what anybody else may think.

Place emphasis on letting your child know that a diagnosis doesn't mean there is something wrong with them; it just means their brain functions differently from non-autistic people. Also, there is nothing wrong with being different, and the different ways of functioning do not automatically mean you will be better or worse at something.

Explain to your child there are thousands and thousands of autistic people in the world. We just don't tend to notice because autism is a hidden condition, not a physical disability. Explain that other people may pick up on their social differences when communicating, or maybe your child has anxiety or meltdowns in public, but that doesn't always mean people will pick up on them being autistic. Helping them deal with the stigma that is associated with being labelled will make it easier for them to accept their autistic identity.

You may find your child already knows deep down that they may be different, especially if they have encountered other autistic children, such as siblings or school friends. They may identify with the similarities in themselves. If your child is curious and asking questions such as, "Is something wrong with me? Why can't I make friends? Why do I struggle in class? Why am I different?"

Use this opportunity to find out their understanding of autism. Helping them to express their difficulties is very important to help you both connect. If the child feels listened to and supported whilst gaining your trust, this gives them reassurance that they can come back to you when they have issues in the future. Avoiding the situation may shut them off.

When trying to explain the autism spectrum, it's not always simple to just give a clear-cut explanation out right. As we know, there are no two autistic people exactly the same. Therefore, not all children will require the same support or present the same characteristics.

There are many children that are assigned a one-to-one support teacher when in school. They may have noticed this and wonder why the other children don't have that support; explaining to them why additional support is put in place is essential to helping them understand their difficulties and needs.

As said before, there are no definitive clear-cut ways that you should use when discussing the diagnosis with your child; but to give you some ideas, I have listed a few below:

- Ensure you have their attention and go to a quiet, comfortable environment with no distractions.
- Ask your child if, and what, they know about autism; it will let you gauge their level of understanding.
- Ask if they feel different to other children, or if they have any struggles or difficulties compared to others. You may know some of those difficulties, so perhaps prompt them by discussing these.

- Explain these difficulties and differences are what makes them autistic.
- Pause. Give them time to think and respond. Try not to overload them too much. Depending on how they react and respond will determine which step you take next.

If the child responds in a defiant manner, doesn't accept the diagnosis or doesn't feel comfortable or happy discussing it, respect their wishes and give them space to process everything. Let them know that if they want to talk about their diagnosis another time or with somebody else, that's totally fine, and there is no pressure.

Perhaps it would sound better coming from a doctor or a teacher or a different family member. The child may just need to learn quietly on their own. There are books, websites and YouTube videos that can be of great help when learning. Ultimately, let it be their choice to decide when and how they will accept their diagnosis.

Children will process stress on all different levels, especially if they are emotionally immature. The stress from taking on this new identity can cause many new anxieties. Think how you felt when you realised your child was autistic; how did *you* process it? Did you internalise it for a while or talk it out with friends and family? Did you have worries, or were you totally fine? Every individual has different coping mechanisms; this is your time to be mindful and recognise how your child copes will differ. I often hear many parents metaphorically say, "The diagnosis hit me like a ton of bricks."

If parents are experiencing this feeling, they have to acknowledge it may hit the child like a ton of bricks too.

I know of lots of autistic adults that have gone through life only ever telling a few people that they are autistic. For them, this is totally fine and how they like it (I am one of those people, too). It lessens their anxiety and allows them to function in society without people judging or focusing on their diagnosis.

If your child accepts and feels comfortable discussing what it means for them to be autistic, consider concentrating on their abilities and positive characteristics first. This will open their mind to see how wonderful they are. Some examples of positives you can say are:

- You are amazing at remembering facts, dates, numbers, etc.
- You have an eye for details, order and repetition.
- You are creative, e.g., arts, music, crafts, building.
- You are trusting and loyal.
- You are very literal and say what you mean.
- You are very caring and amazing with animals.
- You are good with rules, manners and instructions.
- You can focus intensely on specialised subjects/hobbies.

Use this time to create an *autism bond* with your child; a feeling of belonging. Show them you want to learn about their autism too—learning how your child experiences life's difficulties. How they grow, develop and see the world through different eyes.

Make sure your child knows autism is not an illness; there is no special pill that will just take it away. They won't grow out of it either. Instead, they will learn how to cope better in life and discover that they don't need fixing to fit into society; they are not broken — they are how they are meant to be, just perfect.

The more intricate part is talking to your child about their difficulties and the things that society doesn't see as *normal* behaviour. I believe every unfavourable characteristic deserves an explanation.

Example: You have difficulty making friends, maintaining friendships, and playing in groups.

Explanation: You like to play independently, on your own, in your own set way. This is what you prefer, and this makes you happy. It's just that people expect children to have lots of friends and to enjoy playing in groups, this makes you different.

Example: You find it difficult to concentrate whilst in class. You fidget a lot and like to tap or rock constantly.

Explanation: The classroom is a busy environment with lots of uncertainties, noise and disruptions. This distracts you and disrupts your focus. The tapping and rocking soothe you; it's a form of stimming which helps you keep calm. Unfortunately, the teacher doesn't recognise that you are trying to listen and doesn't understand stimming. These are *your* differences that people need to know about you.

Being honest with your child about what makes them different will help them with self-awareness of their characteristics and behaviours when around others.

If you find once you have discussed autism with your child and you are struggling with helping them to understand, there are other options you can look at, such as groups for parents of autistic children/social groups for autistic children. Online courses for parents, books, websites and blogs. The National Autistic Society (NAS) has a wealth of information on their website. They also hold group meetings up and down the country; some areas offer the Early Bird Autism Programme for parents.

Looking back to when my son received his diagnosis (two years old), even though I am autistic myself, I still found it hard-hitting when reading his assessment report. I expected them to diagnose him; there was no denying the fact that my son is autistic. I thought we would receive the diagnosis and assessment report, and after, everything would carry on as usual. It couldn't have been more different.

Initially, there was a huge relief because I knew how important it was for my son to receive a clinical autism diagnosis to help him and us as a family, but I hadn't expected the impact the assessment report would have had on me. It can be very difficult to read specific details about your beloved child in such a derogative manner. To me, my son is perfect. I'm happy that he is autistic, and I wouldn't want him any other way. Yet, this assessment report focused on the things he should be doing and the things he couldn't do. The areas he's fallen behind in and where he needs support to catch up. Naturally, I questioned, *Was it me? What was I doing that was so wrong for this report to point out everything that my child should and shouldn't be doing?*

At the time, I thought to myself, if I find all this difficult to get my head around, how on earth can I expect my son to do the same? My son was non-verbal at the time and very young, so I didn't need him to process or understand what had gone on regarding his diagnosis straight away.

My son was six years old when I first discussed his autism diagnosis with him. One day, out of the blue, he just said, "Mummy, am I autism?" It took me by surprise. I replied, "Do you mean autistic?"

Once I had got over the initial shock, I said to myself, *Okay, I am going to have to do this.*

I took him to a big open field that overlooked trees. It was very peaceful, away from his sibling and other distractions. I started by saying to him, "Do you remember when you were younger, and you struggled with talking? This is why you have help at school. Also, do you remember when you needed to wear ear defenders outside of the house or when I was vacuuming? This is because you have a hearing sensitivity."

We carried on talking about specific things that I knew my son could relate to, then explained this is what makes him autistic. Followed by Mummy is autistic too. I told him which of his family members are diagnosed and discussed autistic celebrities who are on tv that he knew of. I'll never forget his reply, "Does that mean I am autism?"

Discussing other autistic people with him seemed to take away the feeling of being singled out. My son is a visual learner and loves to read, so I got a book specifically for children from the library to help him learn more details about autism (I didn't want to overwhelm him by using too much verbal language). It turned out he loved the book so much that I ended up buying it for him to keep so he could read it whenever he liked. I didn't want to swamp him with too much information, so we didn't go into enormous amounts of detail. I told him that if he had any questions, he just needed to ask, and if he wanted to go on Google or YouTube to learn anything on his own, then that's fine.

After that discussion, we didn't talk about autism again for about four weeks, then he just brought it up and said, "I'm autism, Mummy." I asked him if he'd been thinking about our discussion and if he wanted to learn anything, but he seemed content with just knowing that he's autistic.

As time has gone on, when he is struggling with certain things, mainly language, I will have to put his sentences in the correct order and context. He gets frustrated when he doesn't know the right word to explain something, so I explain it's fine; this is part of being autistic. He seems less frustrated with his speech and has much more patience knowing it's just the way he is. We try not to over emphasise his differences, but rather teach him this is what makes you, *you*, we are all different.

Before my AS diagnosis, I knew there were many things different about me. The way I learnt new things, how I interacted with people, my daily struggles with anxiety, my need for perfectionism and order, my intense interests, and many other reasons.

From the age of eighteen, I have had many counselling sessions to help with my struggles with anxiety and bouts of depression. It was at a routine appointment when a doctor first said to me, "Are you on the spectrum?"

I dismissed it for a long time. Back then, it wasn't common for girls to be diagnosed. The more I learned about ASD, the more I realised it answered many questions about why I had found so many things highly challenging. It was only when I was going through my assessment that I realised what my anxiety was really all about, not realising I had been battling through it daily for years. The clinician who diagnosed me said, "I have never met anyone that masks their difficulties as much as you do. It must be really exhausting!"

She then went into detail, explaining how I had done this and the impact it has had on my mental health. If I hadn't had it explained to me what autism means for me; I don't think I would have grasped it as well as I had. Afterwards, I spent a lot of time reflecting on what had happened in my life because I didn't understand that I was, in fact, autistic; why I failed at school, why I was hopeless when it came to boyfriends, why I had struggled with employment going from job to job, and mostly why

I suffered terribly with anxiety and my mental health.

******

If you are not yet at the stage where your child knows they are autistic, when you are ready, whichever way you decide to tell them, and the approaches you use to help them to understand their autistic characteristics—it's totally your choice how you do it.

There will no doubt be difficulty in explaining what autism is, so try not to put too much pressure on yourself. To make the process easier ensure you put the preparations in place so you can connect with your child and build that autism bond.

Chapter 3

Discussing Your Child's Diagnosis with Family and Friends

When your child goes through an autism assessment or receives an autism spectrum diagnosis, it is common to go to family and friends for support, guidance and assurance. We find that most people in society have heard of autism and know of people that are autistic, but that doesn't necessarily mean that they understand what it means to *be* autistic—and they may not fully grasp your situation.

When you discuss your child, depending on the other person's experience and understanding of your child, it will ultimately impact the way they support you and respond. Some people may be really supportive and understanding and see that your child requires a diagnosis; others may think it's nonsense and dismiss your concerns. Either way, remember, this is *your* child. If people do not respect your choice to pursue a diagnosis for your child, this is where you need to be strong and set boundaries to protect yourself from negative opinions.

You may have a child that doesn't meet the criteria for an ASD diagnosis. But at least you will have answers and peace of mind that you have sought professional help for your child, instead of not knowing, which may subsequently have caused detrimental effects to their well-being and development.

It can be very isolating when people you lean on for support just think you are crazy and overprotective. Even more so when they pass judgment and try to give their own ideas and opinions on how to parent an autistic child. You may find people become *specialists* about your personal situation; when in reality, they have no idea what parents of autistic children endure daily. Sometimes, you just have to admit there will always be people that are ignorant to your situation and will never embrace your child's differences.

I hear all too often parents saying, "I've grown a thick skin and learnt to brush off negative comments and opinions." They learn to repel the ignorance so that it doesn't affect them, avoiding the feelings of bitterness and anger towards them. If they don't, it just becomes exhausting and energy draining.

Reactions and responses that are commonly verbalised by family/friends/society pre and post-diagnosis:

- Are you sure? He doesn't look autistic.
- Oh. What a shame.
- Oh yeah, we noticed!

- Oh dear, but we still love him.
- Why don't you just discipline him and teach him some manners?
- Normal kids do that too.
- He just needs a good slap.
- She just spends too much time playing computer games/watching her iPad.
- He'll grow out of it; it's just a phase.
- Oh, I wouldn't have known.
- She seems fine to me.
- My cousin is autistic, and she's nothing like him, so she definitely can't be autistic.
- Oh, he's just doing it for attention.
- You're just overprotective/over-reacting.
- But he's so smart.
- Well, she makes eye contact, and she looks when I call her name. Are you sure?
- Yeah, I thought so. I knew there was something 'wrong' with him from birth.
- She's just quirky, that's all.
- It's just hormones; my son has meltdowns too.
- It's just learnt behaviour.
- I think he's just a lazy boy; all boys are lazy.
- Well, she doesn't act like that when she's around me. So it must be your parenting.
- Most children have something wrong with them these days.
- Is that a medical illness?

It's natural to take offence to the derogatory comments, but it's important to remember, the way people react and respond is not an accurate reflection of your child; it's their interpretation of autism. You may find their reaction is simply because they don't know how to respond to you.

The comments I commonly get regarding my son are:

- I would never have known he's autistic; he doesn't act like it. He's too well behaved.
- Are you sure, he doesn't look it?
- He must have the mild type because I can't tell.

I've had moments when I've wanted to respond with, *If you only knew about half of what we have been through, you'd soon change your opinion*. But I don't. There's no point. They'll never understand. So I just shrug the comments off. After all, it's just their opinion.

As an adult, when I tell people I'm autistic, I receive totally different comments compared to my child. I tend to typically get comments such as:

- Does that make you really brainy?
- Oh, but you can talk really well.
- How can you be? You're married and have kids.

I have also encountered many people that don't even think I'm autistic, and they'll say that bluntly to my face. They'll judge me based on their experiences of autism, but when they get to know me, and I don't feel I have to mask my autistic characteristics, they're then like, "Oh yeah, I now understand what makes you autistic."

There are many people that will try their best to learn about your child and your situation so they can support you but will still have moments where they just don't understand. It can be frustrating, but just recognise that they are trying, and you may need to be patient. Unless these people spend day in day out with your child, they will more than likely not understand entirely from your perspective.

You'll find a part of your role as a parent of an autistic child is taken up by educating friends and family not just about your child, but autism in general. It can become frustrating when they don't listen and acknowledge your child's specific needs and make you feel completely invalidated because they have no way of understanding the complexities of autism. You may find, even the families that have many autistic diagnosed children in them will still have their own ideas of how your child should be and how you should parent them.

You may have family or friends that want to keep your child's diagnosis a secret, not wanting to tell the neighbours, friends or other family members.

I have heard parents of autistic children say they stopped getting invited to family outings and functions because the family didn't want to deal with their child. For example, he's too hyperactive when in public, has anti-social tendencies or social awkwardness, social outbursts, etc. The family and friends just weren't prepared to make the adjustments. Usually, the parents would hear after the event, "Oh, didn't you get the invite? We sent one out. You must not have received it."

You may find you become estranged from certain friends

and family members—you really find out who cares and who doesn't. In these times, it's good to learn to only concern yourself with those that have direct contact with your child regularly; everybody else, it's just not worth your energy. Do what's best for you and your child. You can pretend to listen and then just let the comments slide.

Remarks voiced by others that are helpful and supportive (and parents would much prefer to hear) are comments such as:

- I'm here for you if you need a break.
- How can I help?
- Is the noise too much? Shall we quieten it down?
- What triggers his anxiety?
- Am I overstimulating him?
- Are there any foods you do not want him to have when he's at my house?
- What are his calming/coping strategies?
- What preparations does he need when doing something new with him?
- Is he okay with change?
- What routines does he have?
- What does he like to talk about?
- What are his special interests?

There will also be times when all you want to hear them simply say is:

- I'm sorry. I didn't realise you needed this support.
- I didn't realise he found things to be this difficult; I now understand.

- Sorry for giving you a hard time with your parenting skills and techniques.

There will be moments when all we need is for someone to just listen. We don't need any advice, no opinions, no answers, just someone to say, *I'm here to listen if you need me*.

When I started writing this chapter, I hadn't realised just how emotional it would make me feel. One of the main emotions I feel when putting it down on paper is loneliness. The loneliness was probably the deepest feeling that overwhelmed me at the beginning of my son's autism journey.

I have had a balance of supportive and non-supportive people in my life since my son was going through the assessment and diagnosis. I can count on one hand the people that supported me and was there when I needed them. The others just didn't spend enough time with my son, so I didn't see the point in trying to explain what life for us was like. Over the years, I have become more vocal about my son and his difficulties; if I hadn't, I don't think people would have understood his differences and specific needs. I've had times when I've even questioned if they honestly care.

I hate to admit it, but there were also times when I just wanted to scream at the top of my voice, WOULD SOMEBODY PLEASE JUST HELP ME!

But I felt silenced. Like nobody was there for me.

This is where parents need to be mindful of their own mental health. It's all too easy to forget about caring for yourself when you have somebody you are caring for that needs you equally, if not more. I hear all too often of parents (especially single parents) suffering from burnout and exhaustion because they don't get any respite. Divorce and temporary separation are common occurrences as well. This is because the changes that an autistic child brings to the family can be too much for a parent or both parents to comprehend.

It's common for one parent to have to stay at home to become a full-time carer, especially with school-age children. Home-schooling is increasing amongst autistic children because of the school system not being able to provide adequate teaching methods and support whilst in school to meet the needs of an autistic child.

An autistic child's behaviour can become out of control, and unpredictable at times. Some children may exhibit violent and aggressive behaviours, especially in the teenage years. Many parents report they have had to call the police to restrain their child, because they don't feel safe in their own home when they are in a state of anger and rage. This is obviously only in severe cases, not all parents will experience these behaviours, but those that do will go through enormous emotional stress and fatigue.

Some parents are put on anti-depressants or other prescription drugs to help them manage the stress. Many turn to self-medicating with alcohol, and other negative coping strategies. I know this may make parenting an autistic child sound negative and torturous, but this is the reality for some parents.

I know only too well the impact parenting an autistic child has on mental health. I have put enormous stress on myself when worrying about my child and trying to understand his specific needs—especially when my son was non-verbal. I constantly questioned myself, *Am I doing this right? Can he understand me? How can I connect with him?*

My world revolved around my child because I didn't feel I could trust anybody else to look after him and understand him like I did. I began to stop caring for myself, stopped exercising, stopped socializing and stopped making an effort with my appearance. I gained weight because food became my emotional crutch when I was feeling lost. I had days when I felt like I wasn't good enough for my child, like I just couldn't understand how to respond to his needs. Many times, I have felt tremendous guilt for feeling like that, and those thoughts can really impact you negatively; but when you don't have the support from family and friends, it can become all too easy to be hard on yourself.

I'm sure most parents of autistic children will be able to list tons of bad days, but there are also just as many good days when you love absolutely everything about autism and what it brings to your child's life. You find yourself celebrating the most random achievements that your child makes. To others, they seem just like any other daily occurrences, but to you, they are huge celebrations.

I couldn't finish this chapter without including autism professionals. After all, parents do tend to spend a lot of time discussing their child with them.

When I say autism professionals, I mean counsellors, psychologists, paediatricians, GP's, speech and language therapists, etc.

There are some amazing service providers and school teachers out there that go above and beyond for our children. Autism services provide a lifeline for autistic families; without these services' autism support, understanding and acceptance within society wouldn't be where it is today. That being said, the quality of these services differs throughout the country. This depends on funding, training, staff management, staff utilisation, staff availability, and so on as to whether you get adequate support.

There's a common phrase in the autism community, *'it's a postcode lottery for those who get the best services.'* Meaning, each county can provide a different kind of support and service than the next county.

The most common controversial aspect when receiving support is how these professionals view autism. I frequently hear of parents being angered when a professional they have put their trust in flippantly says phrases such as, "We're all on the spectrum somewhere, we're all a little bit autistic."

It makes them question how these service providers can help if they're just going to treat them like everyone is autistic.

Autistic adults and parents of autistic children know not *everyone* is a little bit autistic. Whether people think the statement is correct or incorrect, either way, it would be beneficial for professionals to stop saying such things because it is putting autistic families in a position of confusion about what it actually means to be autistic.

When I hear people say that, it makes me think they are not viewing autism from an autistic perspective. It is called the *autism* spectrum for a reason, not the *everybody* spectrum.

It's like me saying to you that I'm a little bit like a dog. Day to day, I walk around on all fours, run around the room barking when the doorbell rings, pant heavily and lie down when I'm hot, cock my leg up against the tree for a wee, you get the gist. If I was to exhibit these traits day in day out, would it make me a little bit of a dog or somewhere on the hound spectrum?

No, I am human and will always function like a human, regardless. So, trying to say everyone is a little bit autistic just because they may have anxiety, be unsociable, like to collect things and be a neat freak, it most definitely does not make them a little bit autistic.

The way autistic people think, communicate and experience the world different to that of non-autistic people is what makes them autistic. Maybe professionals should start saying everybody shares similar personality traits and can exhibit similar behaviours. It's how autistic people respond and react with these characteristics that make them different to non-autistics.

As somebody that is autistic, has an autistic son (and many other autistic family members), has supported many autistic families over the years, plus a first-class degree in Autism: Special Education, it's fair to say I can usually pick up on the professionals that truly don't understand what it means to be on the autism spectrum. Rarely do I meet non-autistic service providers (working within local authorities) that fully understand the differences and what it means to be autistic. However, that doesn't mean the services are useless; far from it, they have made tons of progress in the past decade. I find the services are getting much better at understanding autistic people.

Whilst at university studying autism, a common discussion that would pop up would be that we think there should be at least one adult autistic person employed within these services to help bridge the gap in understanding the complexities of autism.

In my experience, I have rarely had professionals pass judgment on how I should parent my non-autistic daughter, and yet, I get an abundance of opinions and judgment regarding my autistic son. One time I was in a paediatrician's office; he questioned why I was doing something in particular regarding communicating with my son (my son was non-verbal at the time). He also talked down to me and looked at me with an intense look of disgust; it made me feel that as a parent, I didn't know what I was doing because it was my way of doing things and not his.

I began to explain, I'm autistic too, and when I was a child, my younger brother had similar speech delays like my son. So I'd had lots of experience and an understanding of how to help my child.

The paediatrician rudely responded with, "Girls aren't autistic, only boys!" He was clearly an old school doctor and completely ignored the fact that I knew what I was doing and how to help my child.

When you are a parent, and all you're trying to do is the best for your child, and you encounter people like this, remember, they only see a snippet of your life. If they want to talk to you in a patronising manner, don't hesitate to ask to see a different doctor or service provider.

I'm not saying that all services and experiences with professionals are bad, not at all, but over the years and the high number of professional people I've encountered, I can honestly say only about 20% of the services my son and I have received has been positive and useful. Because of these experiences, I started to ask what experience and qualifications the people dealing with my son had. It got to a stage where I felt they were just wasting our time, so I discharged my son from many of the services—this being the reason why I went on to higher education to gain more knowledge, enabling me to become more involved in the autism sector.

Always trust your instincts with people's advice, and if it does not fit your child's needs, don't be afraid to ask questions or request a second opinion. Of course, you can always politely say, "That's not suitable for my child." As a parent, you are there to be the child's voice, their advocate. You know the child better than anybody else; your child needs positive influences, as do you.

Chapter 4

ASD Comorbid Associated Conditions

An autism diagnosis can generate many answers regarding your child's difficulties. You may have also discovered your child has another autistic associated condition(s) (known as comorbid conditions), such as attention deficit disorder (ADD), Rhett syndrome, Irlen's syndrome, pathological demand avoidance (PDA), Fragile X syndrome (FXS), specific learning disability (SLD), dyspraxia, dyslexia and many more. It may be beneficial to research and familiarise yourself with autistic comorbid conditions. Then, if future behaviours or difficulties arise which you can't comprehend, you may then recognise the behaviours as a possible comorbid condition.

Mental health disorders such as different forms of an anxiety disorder, depression, bipolar disorder are also widely acknowledged as comorbid conditions associated with autism. I have found mental health conditions to be an integral part of ASDs. From experience, most adult autistic people that I have encountered have experienced mental health problems at some stage in their life. This can be because of being bullied, not fitting in, struggles related to school and employment, or failing to maintain healthy relationships and friendships. The profound impact these difficulties have on autistic people contributes to why we now see so many autistic adults depending on government funding—such as Personal Independence Payments (PIP) because the mental health aspects associated with autism prevent them from maintaining employment and functioning effectively in their day-to-day life.

If you have an older child, you may find they are already experiencing a mental health condition. In the UK, we have a service provider called Child Adolescent and Mental Health Service (CAMHS). CAMHS work with children that have difficulties with their emotional and behavioural well-being. They have an extensive waiting list for children, just like we see with ASD assessments, and when you get support, it does not guarantee that your child will accept or respond to the recommended treatment or support. Therefore, developing connections with your child is massively important to help you understand how your child is feeling inside, and to recognise when they need you for mental and emotional support.

As a parent, you may find you are already attuned to your child's mental and emotional needs and specific areas of difficulty, and understand how to connect with them. However, many parents will find the whole process of understanding how to support their child to be too overwhelming and complicated; this is because of the many complexities of autism.

When understanding my child, I have always used the approach that he is the teacher and I am the pupil. So to connect with him, I need to listen, observe, learn, take notes, try new things, fail many times and try again. When anyone learns about something new, it takes time, effort and commitment. Just because I'm autistic and involved in the autism sector, it doesn't automatically mean I know everything there is to know about my son's needs. I still need to connect with him on his level and recognise what specifically makes him autistic.

Learning how to support and connect with your child may take weeks, months, or even years. As parents, there is an enormous amount of pressure to get everything right straight away. In today's society, they ingrain it in us to judge ourselves and others, they pilot us daily by the ever-evolving media and social media platforms such as Facebook, Twitter and YouTube. Having a child that is regarded as being different to the typical norm inevitably brings additional challenges to parenting. I have learnt one of the hardest things about parenting an autistic child, is not knowing how to help them. You can have all the love and patience in the world, but if you can't connect and help your child, it can make you feel like a failure.

When connecting with your child, it is important to remember the autistic brain does not have the same development trajectory as the non-autistic brain. They told me to throw out the 'rule book' regarding my son hitting the expected milestones at each developmental stage.

My son didn't start learning how to walk until he was eighteen months old, and he didn't use full reciprocal speech until he was five years old. I learnt early on not to place any expectations on my son's development because if I did, I just knew I was potentially setting him up to fail.

I'm not going to deny, there were times I wished he could talk, it was very difficult, but I resigned myself to the fact he doesn't communicate in a typical way. I realised I would need to find another way to help him interact and understand me and vice versa.

When my son was preverbal, he communicated through noises. Certain cough like sounds would let me know when he was thirsty, or a specific whine would let me know he wanted something. When we potty trained, we used one simple sound that I repeated over and over until he recognised it as a trigger sound to use, to let me know he needed to use the potty/toilet. We also used picture cards and picture boards around the house. I would have pictures of food that he could point to so he could pick what he wanted to eat; I would put a photograph of his toothbrush on the picture board and point to it at bedtime to communicate what was happening, I did the same for bath time, and so on. He had a few easy words that he could say, *oh dear, more, choo-choo*. It took a long time for him to build up this small vocabulary, but those few words opened the communication barriers.

He then learnt he could connect through all of these

sounds, which prompted him to focus more on language. He began to copy words, but for a long time, they had no meaning. For a while, he would say the word *mummy*, but he didn't know what it meant or that I was in fact, Mummy. He'd just heard me saying the word to him lots and learned to repeat it (known as echolalia). Until one day, I was in bed sleeping; I woke to him calling out, "Mummy! Mummy!" He was stood at his safety gate in his bedroom, calling for me. Then when I came, he gave me the biggest smile. I just burst into tears; it was then that I knew he had connected the word to me.

When I realised my son could learn context, I supported him by spending the next two years reading to him day in, day out, teaching him how to associate the words to things and how to use the words in context. Our local library in our town was a life-saver. Each week we would go and pick new picture books together; it brings back beautiful memories. When he picked up new words and phrases that I hadn't taught him, I would say, "Where has he heard that?" Because I knew his limited use of language had mostly come from learning words from me.

I look back and think how I have had to parent and connect with my son in a completely different way compared to my non-autistic daughter. My daughter naturally picked everything up on her own. She would watch and copy everything. She walked at nine months old, talked at eighteen months, could count to ten at two years old; every milestone was surpassed effortlessly. For a typically developing child, it is to be expected.

Being autistic myself and having an autistic child, it

makes you realise your autistic child is developing perfectly fine for their 'typical' developmental trajectory, and that is what makes them autistic.

It makes parenting that much different because we have to learn how to parent the autistic way.

My daughter is nineteen months younger than my son, they don't have the biggest age gap, but even so, you would still think my daughter is the eldest child. So many times I've been asked, "Are they twins?" Because where my son has developed differently, he is delayed socially and emotionally. He's also shorter compared to his peers, so people tend to view him as being a lot younger than he actually is.

Chapter 5

Connecting Through Special Interests

For many autistic people, it is common for them to stay in a childlike state of mind or appear somewhat immature for their age. Childhood interests and memories they have now may still be just as important to them in ten, twenty, thirty+ years. For example, things they like to collect like cars, computer games, Barbie dolls, etc. They may still be very passionate about particular music genres, pop stars and bands, tv programmes, movies, and characters. As parents, we need to bear this in mind and be respectful of their interests; after all, it's what makes them happy.

Not all autistic people will hold on to the same interests. Many will switch them up, constantly changing them, this can be quite frustrating for parents or partners of autistic adults, but many lessons can be learned from these interests.

My son has loved Lego since the age of two (he's now

eight). Lego has helped him to connect with me and others. He's developed many communication skills through this; he specifically likes to build customised vehicles. Lego is all he is interested in, specifically the Lego City range, and he'll only play with that particular range. I've introduced other interests that he can play with so he can see what else is out there, but I realised he just isn't interested. I respect that Lego City is his main focus, and this is what makes him happy, therefore don't try to change him.

We can describe special interests as highly focused (obsessive) activities. They are extremely important to autistic children and adults because many autistic people don't gain connections through people. Instead, they can gain connections through objects, music, tv programmes, computer games, specialised topics of interest, sport, and so on. These interests act as a comfort and a way to relax. They can enjoy them on their own; alone time for autistic people is their haven, their sanctuary. It's a place for thoughts and doing things they love without judgment and interference from others.

Not all autistic children will have special interests; they may fluctuate between different activities or struggle with maintaining attention on one specific area of interest. They can have hobbies such as riding a bike, going to dance groups, karate classes and swimming lessons. They may not become overly focused on them, but a child can still find fulfilment in brief interests.

There will be children that are not interested in anything. I hear parents saying, "Why doesn't my autistic child have a special interest or a talent?" Or "Why isn't my child a savant or gifted like other autistic kids?" It all depends on the child and how they function and connect with the world.

There's a lot of stereotyping with autistic special interests. For example, it's common for trains, computers, science, and maths to be associated with autistic interests and expertise. When in reality, we're not all train spotters, computer geeks, excellent physicists or mathematicians.

I failed terribly at school. I think because, on the whole, I just didn't enjoy learning in large groups and having to join in. As a result, I suffered tremendously from anxiety and struggled to remain focused. Yet I loved all the creative classes like cooking class, textiles and art. Classes where I could work on my own and didn't need to use the theoretical part of my brain, I was better at using my creative side.

My son on the other hand, is very good academically. He loves to learn about facts and history, how things are made and why they work the way they do. He is an amazing reader and good at maths, excellent with computers, yet, he isn't particularly creative like I am. He will do crafts, colour, paint and bake cakes with me, but he very rarely chooses to. He likes to make his brain work and learn new things; I love that we are so different; he teaches me new facts every day.

When I look back over the years at my special interests and how I would like to connect with the world, I have many fond memories of music and handbags. The interest in handbags came because it was what all the teenage girls at that age liked. I felt like, if I liked the same things and looked the same, then I would fit in.

I've always enjoyed learning about fashion but have always been clueless when it comes to being fashionable. This means I have always depended on celebrity and fashion magazines for style ideas and inspiration.

In my late teens, I spent many hours on New Bond Street in London watching people come out of the designer shops with their handbags. I liked to learn the names, the style, the season, the designer, etc. I loved how the bags were made and looked; they were aesthetically pleasing, but I never actually went into the shops. The thought of interacting with the sales people selling these luxury items brought on too much intense anxiety, and I would overthink everything, so I never went in and treated myself.

I have also loved music from a very young age. Back in the early-mid 1980s, my parents only had a tiny black and white television with four channels, so the radio and cassette stereo was on a lot. I also had my very own record player in my bedroom. I loved all the 80s pop stars like Kylie Minogue, Madonna, WHAM!, Whitney Houston and Michael Jackson. Then when I hit my teens in the 1990s, it was all about the boy bands. I was fanatical about PJ and Duncan, Boyzone and Take That (UK boy bands). I spent hours tape recording them when they were on the television, so I could watch them back, over and over (before they invented YouTube). I bought all the magazines, CD's and merchandise, and would go to their concerts. I just felt this immense connection with these strangers.

None of my family understood why I liked them and obsessed over them; they would make fun of me. When I look back to those times, it brings hurtful negative feelings that they judged me so much; they made me feel like I should be ashamed of what I loved and liked to do the most.

As I look back, it makes me question *if they would have tried to connect with me more regarding my special interests, would they have understood me more and have had a better connection with me?* This is why I say it's important to respect your child's interests and, most of all, pay attention to how it makes them feel.

In my 20s, I was pleased to hear that Boyzone and Take That had reformed to make more music and tour. I continued following their music and going to concerts; it was still important to me having that connection.

As I journeyed through life, anxiety and depression had taken over many aspects of my day-to-day functioning. With that, my interests in music shifted; it had now become not just a special interest but more of a healing therapy. That therapy for me came in the name of George Michael—singer and musician. Somehow his music came back to me at a time when I felt alone and overwhelmed with life. I'd grown up with George's music, all the way back into the 1980s when he was in WHAM! and into his Faith era, and so on. He became (and still is) a significant interest that has really brought order to my disordered life. His music calms me when my anxiety is high or when the thoughts are taking over in my mind.

I think because George was a controversial artist who openly wrote about his life and issues with relationships, loss of loved ones, addiction, his sexuality, negative judgement from society, and so on. This, I feel, is what created the connection to him, as if he understands me and the difficulties I endure.

Observing and recognising how your child interacts with their special interests can teach you a lot about how they connect with life. It is common for autistic children to be somewhat introverted and can find maintaining friendships difficult due to their communication differences. Even though they may have these communication barriers, many autistic children still want physical and emotional contact with people (but don't know how).

There are many ways you can help a child connect through an interest without directly having to attain friendships.

Sport, such as football, is a good example (I'm not suggesting you have to do this, or it'll apply to every child). Football not only helps a child to connect with people, but also focuses on physical and mental stimulation and provides a platform for them to express themselves through a passion.

Or, the child may just like to watch the sport rather than play, focusing on a specific football team and the players.

This way, a child has connections with people when playing and/or watching football. The child isn't necessarily using direct communication and social skills when connecting with the players; they are simply following the rules and structure of the game — because of each person having a purpose on the football pitch, and the focus is on working as a team to score a goal.

This allows a child to express themselves through their special interest without overexerting themselves via social communication. Instead, they focus the communication on the given subject, football.

This is just one of many interests that may help a child express themselves mentally, physically and emotionally through indirect connections with people.

Special interests can teach us about many aspects of a child's personality. Such as, can the child balance their special interest with family time, or does their interest take over? Do they have an addictive personality or are they laid back? Do they have more of a take it or leave it personality, not bothered if an interest is taken away, or just don't bother with interests in general.

You can also utilise interests to learn what makes a child respond and react, what prompts conversations, excitement, repetitive behaviours, stimming, calming strategies, meltdowns and aggression. Taking note of these can be vital when understanding your child.

I find I can become overly dependent on my special

interests and have had to learn to recognise when I need to find balance, as it could be all too easy to let them interfere with my married life and children.

I become obsessive and highly focused on my interests when I am feeling low or in a state of mind where I feel I'm struggling mentally and emotionally. This is a huge sign to myself and others that something has triggered me, or I'm not coping with my mental health particularly well.

I don't tend to vocalise my struggles until I'm at breaking point, and even then, I don't express my feelings very well; I just tend to cry lots. These interests help me as a coping strategy rather than a hindrance (I find it's usually people that are the hindrance). The interests keep me functioning within my family unit.

Some people may think, well, we all love certain music and artists as an interest, isn't that just normal? What's different about an autistic special interest is the dependency that is placed on it. Like a drug, if it was to be taken away, it would affect how you function daily and how you regulate your emotions and your thought process. You rely on that interest for connection, stimulation, focus, feelings of empowerment, and joy. Therefore, it's not just an interest; it can also function as a coping mechanism. The interest gives us the connections that a parent or friend simply can't.

Interests can also come with drastic changes; this can also impact the way a child functions and connects with people. For example, many children these days are interested in computer games. Computer games provide enormous visual, mental and emotional stimulation. Again, it's an interest that allows a child to play and focus by themselves, without social interaction. If a particular game they are playing becomes too difficult, or the parent changes how long they can play for, or limits the child's playing to certain days and times. When these changes are not implemented through the child's choice but an external factor, this may impact the child's functioning, resulting in behaviour differences.

Therefore, it's important to help a child adapt in these types of situations. Teach them to recognise that changes in life are unavoidable and sometimes happen for a particular reason, which is commonly out of our control.

The preparation the parent puts in place is vital when helping the child to adapt. If the adult is making the changes regarding a special interest, it's the adult who needs to explain the reasons and state exactly what, why, and how you will make the changes. Most importantly, ensure the changes are consistent. Don't say one thing one minute, then do the opposite a day later. This will not help a child learn how to adapt.

When I was younger, my mum was always very good at teaching me how to adapt (even though, back then, I wasn't diagnosed autistic yet). My mum was a very well-organised lady and liked things to be done in particular ways. She was strict with rules and boundaries and always ensured I stayed within them, just like most people would when teaching or disciplining any child. This taught me how to adapt to the family's routines and daily occurrences.

As an adult, inevitably, I still find changes occur regarding my special interests. In my case, sadly, George Michael passed away on Christmas day in 2016. Even though I didn't know him personally, I have frequently visited his home in Oxfordshire (UK) since his passing.

Seeing the tributes and flowers that have been left by fans, all laid down by his front door, is heart-wrenching. But, visiting his home is a way to feel like I can connect with him, somewhere where he loved to be. Some may call it obsessive and eccentric, but for me, it's showing my appreciation to a man that has had such a positive impact on my mental health and well-being. He's also brought an enormous amount of joy into my life through his music.

I'm fortunate that I have an amazing husband who truly understands what having an autistic special interest like George Michael means to me. My husband even supported me whilst I paid my respects at George's house on Christmas day (the anniversary of his passing).

I pass George's home when travelling to visit family, and I like to stop by and spend fifteen minutes with other fans who also have the same gratitude for him and truly understand why it's important to visit and feel connected.

This is when you realise that it has become more than an interest; it's a part of you that helps you to function. I look back to the hours I'd spent on New Bond Street in London, and again, it is all about feeling some sort of connection, being understood, and most of all having a feeling of fitting in without having to have an involvement with people that don't understand you.

I'll never meet George Michael or have all those handbags, but what my special interests give me is personal connections and feelings of contentment. I live in my own happy bubble with my social norms because it keeps me functioning, and to me, that's my normal.

So, it really is important to connect and try to understand your child through THEIR interests, the things that make them happy and recognise how they respond to those interests. It enables you to enter their world and view how they relate to their surroundings—even if it's something as simple as stacking bricks or laying cars in a line. Get down on the floor with them and build, line them blocks up, feel their excitement when those bricks fall over or cheer when they line those cars up beautifully in order.

Appreciate their joys and comforts and respect what they love. This way, you can enter their thoughts, feelings, what stimulates them, calms them, what stresses them, and most of all, what they are gaining and learning from their individual unique experiences in life.

Allowing a child to use self-expression may reveal many hidden skills. For example, they may have an excellent eye for detail, have an amazing memory for keeping facts, be very good at problem-solving and seeing the bigger picture, build and create exciting things, and absorb information quickly. Whatever it may be, don't let being autistic (doing things differently) hold them back.

Holding grudges is a known common autistic characteristic. These grudges can last for years and years. The last thing you want is for your child to blame you for not showing an interest in what makes them happy, and more importantly, autistic. Grudges can create many blockages in mental health and daily life in general. Let their interests help them deal with their overactive minds and put their minds to use doing what they love. I like to think of it as:

> If the brain needs to be chattering all day, every day, then give the brain something to chatter about.

Chapter 6

Helping Your Child Explain Their Autism

One of the most common questions I hear parents ask is, "How do I help my child explain to others that they are autistic?"

When I think about how I tell people that I'm autistic, I don't have one set way of doing it. It all depends on who I am telling and why I am telling them. My personal circumstances rarely require me to have to inform people, but when I do, there are many questions I ask myself:

How do I explain it? How will the person react and respond? Do my friends *really* need to know? What if they change how they are towards me afterwards? Will they think I'm odd?

This is one area that I definitely think needs thoughtful preparation. Preparing your child for when they need to explain that they are autistic to others can be highly beneficial to them and help relieve associated anxieties.

However, how to teach them how to do this can be the tricky part.

Let's say, if you were to ask ten people to explain the autism spectrum or what it means to be autistic, you would no doubt receive ten different explanations. Why? Because there are so many factors to consider when defining and describing autism, for example:

- Age
- Level of maturity
- Comorbid/mental health conditions
- Gender
- Environmental factors
- Support network
- Behaviour/personality
- Language, communication and social abilities/disability
- Sensory processing differences
- Auditory processing differences
- Specific repetitive behaviours/routine/stimming
- Coping strategies/special interests

These are just some things you would need to consider when explaining autism.

Your child may already be at an age where they are comfortable enough to have already told friends about their autism diagnosis and be at ease with doing so, which is a massive step in their development. Being able to effectively communicate what a diagnosis is, typically applies to older children (youths and teenagers, it also depends on their developmental trajectory and their use of social skills). They may already have an awareness of their differences and might feel that they want to discuss their autism with others.

Preschool and younger primary school children may have not yet gained the knowledge to be able to effectively communicate what autism is.

You may be a parent of a child with noticeable differences, i.e., a language/speech impairment, learning disability, requires one-on-one support in school, or attends a specialised school. In these circumstances, it may be apparent to others and not necessary for your child to inform them that they are autistic.

For parents of children that haven't yet approached telling their friends, it may be beneficial to have a little discussion to find out if your child is ok with doing so and get an idea of if, how, and when they want to tell their friends so you can support them.

It's important to let your child know their friends and other children might not fully understand what autism is. So if they tell their friends, the response they get, more than likely, may be unpredictable. Children tend to be blunt and don't filter their responses like adults might. Their response could be really positive or highly offensive, or they might just not respond at all.

To begin with, it may be wise to let your child only tell a few of their friends that they can trust and know on a personal level. This way, their friends will better understand your child and hopefully be a good supportive helper.

To lessen the angst, ask your child what they want to tell people about their diagnosis. What do they feel comfortable saying? Depending on your child and their personality, how they communicate and how they view themselves will ultimately impact how and what they want people to know.

When helping your child learn how to explain autism to others, it's important to let your child know that autism is known as an autism spectrum disorder—because autism has a vast range of characteristics. This means autistic people have different levels of abilities and difficulties, so they are all individuals.

Teaching them to say *I'm autistic* will inform somebody that they have an autism spectrum disorder, but it doesn't explain *what autism means specifically for that child*.

I frequently emphasise '*what autism means specifically for your child*' throughout this book because what you teach your child now about being autistic, will be just as important, if not more, when they are adults.

Yes, most people will have heard of autism and have their own interpretations of what autism is. They may have also had their own experiences with lots of other autistic children. Still, the point is, your child needs to know how to stop themselves from being stereotyped and understand how to explain the specific details specific to them. That will also prevent them from being stigmatised and misunderstood.

As an autistic adult, I've learned that having a communication difference can already put you at a disadvantage when making friends, going for job interviews, etc. But, telling another adult you are diagnosed autistic can make matters even harder. Because nine times out of ten, it totally changes other people's perceptions of you. Just by expressing you have a recognised difference or disability, unless they know you extremely well, they will undoubtedly be inquisitive of your abilities, difficulties and differences. Telling somebody you are autistic in today's society undeniably adds to your character description, and that's what makes us different. Thankfully, I've mostly received positive responses when telling friends. It's usually people that I don't know who make random remarks.

My knowledge of my autistic characteristics is what prepares me to tackle these impromptu situations.

A brief way of describing ASDs can be defined as:

- A differability.
- A different way of functioning/thinking.
- My brain works differently.
- A different operating/processing system.
- A different way of being.

Even though the descriptions are correct, they are vague and don't provide detailed explanations. However, they are good descriptions for autistic people to use when they want to be brief—without divulging copious amounts of information about what makes them autistic.

A good way to help your child explain autism is to provide them with a social script, something they can memorise. A social script will provide a prepared verbal description, so if they are unexpectedly put on the spot, the script they learn will help them deal with the situation. Focus on the points that your child can relate to the most.

These are a few examples that could be used when your child tells someone they are autistic:

- It means I understand and respond to some things differently compared to other children.
- I'm good at schoolwork but not very good at understanding people. It means I get confused a lot in social situations.
- I overthink everything. I struggle at making decisions; it causes me lots of anxiety, which stops me from doing things. That's why I need help sometimes.
- I'm shy with other people. Of course, I like to have friends, but I don't need lots of friends like other children; I have my special interests that make me very happy.

If your child has limitations when communicating verbally, you could put together a visual aid, such as a booklet with specific details for others to read about your child.

For example, your child may have limited language, but they are very attentive and can understand everything other people say. In the book, you could write something like, *Children and adults can talk to and play with me; just because I don't respond verbally doesn't mean I'm not listening and not understanding you.*

Write down likes and dislikes, what triggers and calms your child, also, specific routines, sensory difficulties, and so on. This book can then go to nursery/school, with family members, etc. As the child adapts and develops, the book can evolve too.

Depending on your child's communication abilities, age, maturity, level of autism understanding, and awareness of their needs will ultimately determine what and how your child will describe what autism means for them.

When carrying out research for my dissertation at university, I asked a large number of autistic adults what their experiences were like when making friends with other autistic people and informing them they are also autistic. All of them replied with similar responses, stating they were better understood and didn't experience being judged or treated differently. They were better accepted and felt like they could relax and be themselves. They didn't feel they had to be aware of their differences or hide them (by masking their autistic characteristics). When autistic children and adults mix together, it is a great way to learn and let children see that their differences aren't actually that different when they are with other autistic people. It's a great way to let them learn about themselves from different perspectives and experiences to gain a deeper understanding of autism in general.

When I'm with other autistic adults, even when I tell them I'm autistic, I still have to say which areas I struggle with, especially regarding communication. I find myself saying, "I'm too shy to join in," or "I'm not confident enough to talk in groups where I don't know everyone yet." I like to put it out there because I often think my communication barriers make me appear ignorant or disinterested. I don't want people to think I'm this way because I don't like them or because I'm being rude. It's just my specific communication style. I know I have difficulties with social anxiety, and if I let that anxiety take over, I tend to go mute and unable to let the words come out at all. This is why I have had to learn to be mindful of my areas of limitation and express what I find difficult.

Through experience, when trying to explain autism to others, I have found the biggest misconception surrounding autistic people is associated with learning disabilities. Yes, many autistic people have learning disabilities, but there are also just as many that don't. In fact, many autistic people have above average intelligence and are incredibly creative.

Autism is defined in the DSM-V as a neurodevelopmental condition. Maybe this is where a lot of confusion stems from when trying to understand what it means to be autistic. Being diagnosed with a neurodevelopmental condition doesn't necessarily mean you will have a specific learning disability. I think it's also important to understand this aspect of autism when helping your child understand their diagnosis. Autism teams who diagnose ASD rarely focus on this area; therefore, they don't always provide information or support families to help prevent this huge perplexity when understanding their child post-diagnosis.

It could also explain why I have experienced many people misjudge my diagnosis of autism. I say to people, "I don't have an intellectual disability, so I talk fluently with intellect. It's the way I communicate with others that makes me autistic. I also have no learning disabilities; therefore, I manage adequately in society without assisted support."

My son isn't at the stage yet where he can understand all the autism terms and how to describe what exactly makes him autistic. As I teach him more and more about himself, i.e. what he does that's viewed as different, areas he needs support, and so on, I try to explain that other children won't quite understand his differences, so we don't need to tell them just yet. I also don't think my son is mature enough to make the decision to tell his friends just yet.

My son is fortunate that he has a one-to-one support assistant at school, she helps bridge the communication gaps, but I know she won't always be there to support him in school. So, now that my son understands language, we can build up our discussions over time and slowly prepare how to explain what it means for him to be autistic.

Parents also need to be mindful of how and what they tell other people about their child's diagnosis.

If your child is at a stage where they are coherent and responsive to your conversations with other people, they might hear you talking about them and their diagnosis; it will undoubtedly raise questions. So, it's important to always be mindful about how you talk about your child and discuss their autistic characteristics.

Chapter 7

Teaching Your Child to Advocate Their Needs

Due to the diverse communication differences and developmental variances associated with ASDs, there will be occasions when your child needs to recognise when they need to ask for support. Or, vocalise that they may not understand a situation or perhaps when people misunderstand them. This is known as self-advocacy.

Providing the foundations of self-awareness and how to advocate for themselves will provide valuable benefits throughout life.

Not everyone in society will know what it feels like to be autistic; only an autistic person can tell you that. Yet, it's common to have non-autistic people telling those on the spectrum how they should act and behave. For example, how to make eye contact, be more sociable, be less inappropriate, stop obsessing over things, etc.

When in fact, what they should do is observe the child to

gain a deeper understanding, and if possible, ask the child why they do things the way they do.

Are there sensory aspects, miscommunication, anxieties, etc?

If we don't give the child an opportunity to understand themselves or recognise why they have reacted or responded in a particular way, then they won't identify when they need support, and most importantly, how to ask for help.

There have been times when I have walked out of doctor's appointments with my son because I didn't like the manner they would use when trying to engage with him. Almost every single doctor (and speech therapist) that we have seen has focused on making my child make eye contact when communicating with them.

I understand eye contact is important for many reasons regarding communication, but not one professional explained to my son why they were making him do it. Nor did they consider explaining to me what they intended to achieve by doing this (I think parents should have informed explanations as to why and what the doctor is doing with their child).

If they had sat my son down and said *I need you to look at me so you can recognise and respond to my body language, facial expressions, and so on,* then fine, there would have been an explained purpose for my son to do this. But, still, they provided no logical reason (informing him) so that my son would know why he was being forced to do something he clearly found difficult.

This is what the doctors were missing; they hadn't provided a logical foundation for my child to learn or understand why he needed to utilise this 'typical social skill' that typically comes naturally to non-autistic people.

Providing logical explanations before supporting and treating autistic people should be basic practice, but many professionals seem to neglect this. This can create many communication barriers because an autistic person may misunderstand the doctor's intentions and won't know what questions to ask regarding the given situation. Because of that, they won't know how to advocate for their needs.

Being the primary carer for my son (and being autistic), I know exactly why he doesn't make eye contact and why the doctor's invasive approach was unsuitable. Thankfully, I'm there to advocate for him. Unfortunately, at his age, he doesn't know how to do this yet. Therefore, in these circumstances (where people do not understand his needs), I can use these situations to teach him what to say and do, and how to express himself if he misunderstands what is expected of him.

There will be times when your child simply cannot explain or advocate what they need or why they have reacted in a particular way, because frankly, they just don't know why or how to. This is when we need to step in and prepare them.

For example, let's say an autistic child is in a swimming

lesson with ten other non-autistic children and the swimming teacher shouts, "On my whistle, I want you all to get into the water!" All the children have armbands on to help them float, and the water isn't particularly deep. The whistle blows, and all the children except for the one autistic child jump in. This child suffers terribly from anxiety and unpredictability. Some key points that could be evaluated from this scenario are:

- Does the instructor know the child is autistic?
- Does the child have a water sensitivity?
- Has the child been in the swimming pool before?
- Can the child learn in groups?
- Can the child process the teacher's voice (to learn how to swim) in the echoed environment with water swishing and other disruptive noises?
- Is the temperature too hot/cold for the child, causing sensory issues, triggering additional anxiety?
- Is the child already in a heightened state of anxiety before going to the swimming class?

The child may have many thoughts or questions as a result of their anxiety, such as:

- Is the water going to go on my face/ears/hair?
- What if I can't float?
- Am I going to get splashed?
- What if I can't swim?
- How do I get out of the water?
- Will the teacher help me?
- What if the children look or laugh at me?

The ten other children have got into the water without

hesitation, not even contemplating a single thing. They are enjoying being in the water and splashing around.

Thankfully, this autistic child has had the support put in place. The parent had taken the child to the swimming pool before with the family on a quiet day and familiarised the child with the surroundings. They informed the swimming teacher of the child's needs. The child knows he struggles in the water, therefore, knows he needs to tell the teacher when he needs help. The teacher knows the child is autistic and may need help to get into the pool.

When the whistle blows and the autistic child is there, standing at the side of the pool—having all these apprehensive thoughts running through his mind. The teacher knows to ask the child how he can be of assistance and helps ease the child's anxiety—not forcing him to jump in with the other children, allowing the child to get in the water his way.

The key points are, the parent, swimming teacher and child have worked together to put sufficient support in place, providing the foundations for the child to advocate his needs. The child knows to say things such as:

- I have sensory difficulties with water.
- Learning in a group environment makes me feel anxious because I don't have control of my space.
- If the children come near me, it will worsen my anxiety, but I'm okay if I can go at the end of the line where I can spread out further away if I need to.

If the autistic child had had no preparations put in place (teaching the child self-awareness of his needs and how to speak out for help) prior to the lesson, and if the swimming teacher had very little knowledge regarding autism or the child's specific needs, then this child would have been left in an extremely vulnerable position. They could have left him kicking and screaming at the side of the pool, overly scared, then more than likely been coerced into getting into the pool with no support. This could have caused further anxiety with water and learning how to swim. Learning how to swim is very important regarding the child's safety in the water. Advocating his needs reduces the pressure and allows the child to learn in his specific way, allowing him to have fun and play with the other children.

A child will experience many critical moments in life, which requires them to understand their autism (what makes them different and their areas of difficulty). The complexity of an autistic child's own specific communication style will undoubtedly impact the way they ask for help and support. A child needs to learn the best way for them to express and advocate their needs. Whether this is vocal, using hand and sign language signals, picture cards, certain trigger words, whichever it may be, ultimately, the more you prepare them now, the easier it will become as they get older.

A key factor to consider when helping a child to advocate their needs is how they use expressive language. Are they direct? Or do they use fifty words or more to ask for something when they could have used a simple ten-word sentence? The autistic communication differences can cause huge misunderstandings, especially when the child doesn't recognise that they communicate differently.

An autistic child may not automatically pick up on their differences independently; they will need external input to teach them. This is what makes autistic children different to non-autistic children. Non-autistic children tend to adapt and learn social cues and skills on their own.

A child won't always know how to put sentences together themselves so they can ask for help; we can teach them to say simple things, for instance:

- I don't understand.
- Please, can you help me?
- I need that explanation again; it didn't make sense to me.
- I don't know what you want me to do.
- I'm shy, can you help me join in with the group, please.
- The noise is too loud.
- Everything around me is making me feel anxious; I need a quiet calm environment.
- I get distracted easily; I need help to stay focused.
- Please don't touch me or come too close; it makes me feel uncomfortable.

You may be able to teach an autistic child their differences in communication or how to interact effectively, but it doesn't mean to say they will be able to implement what they have been taught in their day-to-day interactions with others. What it does is provide awareness and acceptance of these differences.

Many autistic children will shut off and struggle to communicate when they feel distressed or put in a difficult situation. Emotions can go from one extreme to another, just fine one minute, then totally explosive the next.

I have lost count of all the different ways I have tried to help my son learn how to recognise when he needs to tell an adult he needs help or is having difficulty of some sort. No two situations are ever the same. When my son is distressed, he will typically shut down. He mostly doesn't know how to explain why and what has upset him. I've had to teach him how to calm himself, so he can then tell me little bits of what has upset or frustrated him. I then have to try to piece everything together. The more I teach him and show him how to ask for help, the better he has become.

My son's one-to-one support assistant will use drawings (social stories) whilst in school to explain certain situations that he's misunderstood, and how he needs to ask for help next time something similar happens. It's taken many months to get to the stage where my son understands why he is being shown how to ask for help. Because of that, he now understands how much it helps him when he advocates his needs. Thankfully this has reduced his frustration and miscommunication with other children and members of staff.

I know my son will need continuous support in this area, as will many autistic children, but the fact is, the support he receives now is helping him progress, and I know he will only get better and better at understanding how to ask for help.

When helping children practice using social skills to advocate their needs, try to put them in a situation or environment that will implement these skills; some examples:

When in a shop or a store, ask your child to ask a member of staff for help when looking for specific items to buy. It'll build confidence when talking to strangers in a controlled environment. If the child gets nervous or doesn't feel comfortable interacting with the shop assistant, you can explain to your child that it's the shop assistants' job to assist you with your purchase. If the child has social awkwardness or feels they have made a social mishap, tell them the shop assistant will most likely forget because they see hundreds of people throughout the week (unless you visit the shop frequently), so the shop assistant will more than likely forget your child. Plus, adults are more inclined to help children, so it's good to develop these skills as early as possible.

Talking on the telephone can be a good way to help your child practice expressing their needs when talking to family or friends. They can say, "I don't understand what you are saying. Can you explain it, please?"

Many autistic people don't know when it's their turn to talk, especially when talking on the phone and can't see the other person because they have no social gestures or clues; they have to focus on their voice, this can be difficult for some. An example, some may need to say, "I'm not being rude; I don't realise when I need to talk, or when I talk too much, or when I should let you have a turn to talk."

The child doesn't necessarily need to change how they are communicating. They just need to explain how they use communication so the person they are talking to can help, instead of getting bored or offended that they never seem to have any conversational flow back and forth.

As an adult, we use the telephone for many things not just talking to friends and family, but also when making appointments, booking a taxi, or ordering takeaway food, etc. A child can practice these skills and recognise if they need help in certain areas, so in the future, when they use the telephone as adults, they can express their difficulties, e.g., "Hi, just so you know, using the phone makes me anxious, sorry, please bear with me." Teach the child not to be embarrassed about asking for help or when asking people to be patient with them.

When your child stays with other people, e.g., grandparents, inevitably, there will be changes to your child's routine and environment. You need to ask yourself, is your child prepared for these changes? Can your child self-advocate when you are not there? If not, preparations need to be put in place both with the child and the grandparents. If you do this from the start, it will help to lessen the child's difficulties.

Teaching your child how to self-advocate from an early age is also very important for their independence and will most definitely help the child later in adulthood and in many aspects of their life. Practising self-sufficiency in daily tasks will prevent them from becoming somewhat dependent on family members and friends. It'll give them confidence when living on their own in adulthood, dating, learning to drive, going to the doctor's office when ill, etc., enabling them to live a fulfilled life.

Understandably, we can't prepare a child for every given situation, but we can prepare them to understand their areas of difficulty, when they are struggling and when and how to ask for help.

Chapter 8

Stressors and Triggers

One of the biggest hurdles parents typically encounter is—recognising and understanding which emotional, mental and physical stressors and triggers (STs) impact their child daily. We can describe stressors as the emotional response to an environmental or external stimulus. Similarly, a trigger is something that causes you to function and respond in a particular way.

We can describe examples of autistic stressors and triggers as:

- Sensory overload (e.g., adverse reactions to loud noises, bright lights, strong smells).
- Over-stimulated (e.g., overloaded with information).
- Social burnout (e.g., exhausted from trying to maintain communication when in groups of people).
- Miscommunication (e.g., not being able to effectively express their feelings).

- Environmental triggers (e.g., anxious when in overcrowded busy places).
- Overthinking everything they do (prevents them from functioning effectively).
- Need for specific routines and structure (become highly agitated when experiencing change).

The examples shown above are just a few of the contributing factors which can produce an array of STs, all of which will be unique to the person. For example, STs can provoke meltdowns, stimming behaviours, anxiety, depression, anger and aggression, self-harming behaviours, withdrawal behaviours, vocal outbursts, and so on.

The level of impact these stressors and triggers have on an autistic person can be determined by many key factors, such as:

- Can the person communicate effectively?
- Does the person recognise what causes their stressors and triggers?
- Does the person have support in place to help calm and control them?

If an autistic child doesn't recognise their stressors and triggers or know how to use calming and coping strategies, it could negatively impact their long-term emotional health and well-being. Therefore, it is important to teach the child to recognise their personal stressors and how to use calming and coping strategies specific to their needs so that they can learn how to self soothe and regulate their emotions when in a state of panic and distress.

To help both you and your child have an awareness and a deeper understanding of what calming and coping strategies they need, you must observe and communicate with your child. Show them you recognise that they struggle with certain aspects and that you are there to help them.

If your child has limited speech or is unaware of their STs, this is where you as a parent need to step in and play the role of a detective, trying to figure out what causes your child's distressed reactions and responses.

If your child is at an age where they can sit down and communicate effectively, it's a good idea to sit down together and discuss what they understand about their stressors and how they respond. If your child can write, you can engage their attention and thoughts by asking them to write down what stresses them the most; this can give you a clear understanding from their perspective. If they struggle to provide logical answers, help them by prompting them (if you know some of their STs). You could write down what you think triggers your child, compare the lists and see if you are both recognising the same issues. This will give you a good sign of what changes need to be made.

An example, a parent may write:

School mornings are difficult. I need to assist and refocus my child, encouraging him to finish eating his breakfast and to get dressed. Most days, we experience meltdowns which makes us late for school. This causes additional stress before the school day has even started.

The child may write:

Getting up in the morning makes me feel stressed. I don't like school; the playground is too loud and crowded with children running around and parents chatting. I worry about who I will play with or talk to. I don't have many friends. The main friend that I do have goes off and plays in groups with all different children. I don't like it when they are like that. I want to play with just my friend and no one else. It makes me feel upset.

There are two different responses, but both are triggered by the same stressor - school. The child is not motivated to go to school; the anxiety starts as soon as the child wakes up. This is causing them to become distracted, unmotivated and uncooperative. When the child is late for school, they are avoiding the chaos of the playground. This is helpful for the child, but it causes additional issues because they are late for school. The friend situation is something that a parent can now discuss and find out how to put coping strategies in place.

Your child's STs will no doubt change over time; keeping a record of the stressors will help you look back and see how things have changed, what's worked or what has gotten worse.

If the child's main stressor is a sensory difficulty, you may find this is the root cause to a lot of additional triggers. For example, if a child has auditory (sound processing) difficulty with certain noises, such as the vacuum cleaner, washing machine, radio, hair dryer, traffic noise, beeping noises in shops, etc. Then this will no doubt cause great distress and additional anxiety when leaving the house, trying new toys and games, visiting other people's homes, etc. A coping strategy to help the child reduce the external noises and control their environment could be something as simple as giving the child a pair of ear defenders or headphones with music when in and outside the home. We can teach a child to put their hands on their ears when the noise is too much, so the caregiver has an indication and can recognise when the child is distressed, enabling them to remove the child from the situation. Recognising the child's needs, providing the child with self-awareness of their auditory triggers, and giving them sufficient coping strategies will help them deal with unpleasant (triggering) noises in the future—reducing additional stressors and associated anxieties.

Autistic children may use 'sensory seeking' as a calming strategy. For example, they may feel the need to be constantly snuggled into a parent or need to feel light pressure on them (especially when trying to self soothe or sleep). Weighted blankets are an excellent aid for helping children with this sensory aspect.

Other sensory seeking activities could be:

- Constantly walking back and forth or in circles.
- Rocking incessantly.
- Needing to make or hear loud noises.
- Have a need for strong familiar smells.

- Chew on non-food items such as clothing or their fingers.
- Want to be constantly touching and picking up objects.

Children can also exhibit sensory avoidance behaviours, such as:

- They don't enjoy being touched, hugged or kissed.
- They don't like labels, certain clothing fabrics or water touching their skin.
- They don't like a certain food or drink texture.

Other sensory aspects to remember. A child may:

- Have limited spatial awareness; clumsy, bump into things.
- Hear certain background noises and experience smells that others don't acknowledge.
- May experience temperature (too hot or cold) differently when compared to others.
- Have specific food tastes, e.g., can only tolerate bland foods.
- Have an infatuation with cleanliness/germs, needing to wash their hands or change their clothes constantly.

Anxiety is a huge sign that your child is experiencing stressors or triggers. This anxiety may present as tummy upset, stress headaches, clinginess, unusual changes in behaviour, vocal tics, aggression. However, in my experience, the biggest cause of anxiety is when the child is taken out of their comfort zone. For example:

- When separated from their parent or support network (at school, going to a family's house, after-school activities, etc).
- If we change their routine or if there is no routine in place (unpredictable environment, need consistency).
- When we put expectations on the child without preparations, e.g., expect them to do something new on their own without support.
- When we put the child in an unfavourable social situation requiring them to interact (especially when in groups or talking to new people).
- When travelling somewhere new. The child may need visual images of the location and an explanation of what will be there/will happen on arrival.

Calming and coping strategies.

Putting in preparations and recognising your child's needs will reduce many triggers and stressors. Similarly, calming and coping strategies are equally important.

We can find these coping strategies in the form of objects, such as a favourite toy, blanket, books and clothes. A child may become overly attached to the object. It can make them feel calm, safe and happy.

Your child may already use calming and coping strategies without even realising, such as:

- Humming to themselves when the noise is too loud/unbearable (the humming sound blocks the noises out).
- Tapping their chest, flapping their hands or making movements that help them feel calm.
- Organise and placing things in order (find things to take control of, shift their thought process).
- Collect specific items which hold significant importance to them (gives them an area of focus).
- Count certain objects over and over/or repeat words.
- Colouring, painting or writing.
- Watching the same movie or listening to the same song over and over.
- Sitting under a blanket or in a dark, quiet room (play tents are useful as a calming tool).

Many autistic people will find the best way to calm themself is when they are in their own environment, with their own familiarities and comforts. They don't always require personal connections with people; they may prefer animals, reading, watching television, playing computer games—basically anything that doesn't require any social interaction. They will like to be left on their own because the social interactions are what cause the additional stressors.

Play therapy is a proven method that can help children to adjust to certain stressors. For example, when implementing techniques such as Lego play, Play-Doh, building bricks, board games, and so on. Children can learn how to take turns, adapt in new situations, recognise and respond to different emotions, use verbal and non-verbal communication skills, and manage and express their feelings.

Fidget toys also provide calming techniques, such as spinning toys, moulding putty, stress balls, fidget cubes, etc. These redirect the child's focus; the fidgeting acts as a form of stimming to help them feel calm.

Practising mindfulness is now becoming a popular calming therapy used with both children and adults. Mindfulness techniques include strategies that calm the mind and body, such as deep breathing, yoga, meditation, carrying out self-love, care and acceptance.

Mindfulness isn't necessarily successful with all children. Especially those who have difficulty following instructions, focusing their attention, and sitting still for long periods of time. It is something that would need patience and practice. However, that's not to say it can't be useful. We know mindfulness has great benefits that can improve the way you feel about yourself and help to clear the mind of negative thoughts and disruptive patterns.

The positive aspects that your child can gain from recognising their stressors and triggers include:

- Greater self-esteem and confidence (helping them to focus on their strengths).
- Self-acceptance of areas of difficulty and limitations (e.g., acknowledge they are socially awkward, and it's okay for them to make social mishaps).

- Can provide awareness for when they may need support from a teacher, parent or service provider.
- Will help them connect with people/maintain healthy friendships and relationships.
- Will have a greater understanding of why they react and behave in certain ways.
- Teach them self-control.
- Experience greater quality of life with reduced anguish.

It is important to enforce positive coping and calming strategies not only to improve mental health and well-being but to also prevent negative unhealthy addictions.

There is a fine line between practising self-care and the things we use as a vice. For example, if a child was to play a computer game for an hour a day to relax and unwind then continue other activities on their own or with the family, the computer game won't necessarily impact the child's conduct. If a child was to play for five hours a day, yes, they may find it pleasurable, but it may become somewhat excessive and cause issues within the family unit.

As a parent, it can be tough trying to teach your child balance and how to recognise impulsive behaviours. After all, they are still children; they are not mini-adults, so they don't have self-control like an adult might. Healthy habits and behaviours have to be reinforced from a young age; otherwise, unhealthy activities and patterns of behaviour might become difficult for them to regulate later in life.

Taking notes or keeping a diary of your child's stressors and triggers can be helpful when trying to recognise specific behavioural patterns—recording what helps or makes things worse. For example, do certain foods make them hyper or anxious? Is a sibling, parent or friend triggering them? Keeping track and recording the stressors and calming strategies can be helpful when relaying information to a teacher or a doctor. Or when you are trying to help family members understand why your child responds and reacts the way they do.

If the child is at nursery or school, ask the teacher if they recognise any particular stressors regarding your child, and if they have found anything that helps to calm them.

You can cross-check each other's experiences and have consistency in your child's support. The common factors can then be emphasised when helping your child transition to new situations and environments, such as new teachers, classes, or school.

Chapter 9

Autistic Behaviours

Prior to the increase in better autism awareness and understanding, autistic children were commonly viewed as uncooperative, unruly, naughty children. The public's perception and misunderstandings were probably the results of limited experience, information, and accurate descriptions of what it actually means to be on the autism spectrum. In the past, television shows and the media tended to show autism in the most severe cases—where comorbid conditions such as intellectual disability and learning disability weren't taken into consideration.

We now see characters such as Sheldon Cooper from the tv show The Big Bang Theory being stereotyped as a typical autistic person. The writers of the show haven't specifically 'labelled' Sheldon autistic. The viewers have recognised his differences in behaviour, seeing he doesn't fit the stereotypical norm. Sheldon Cooper's behaviours show his rigid thinking, inability to change, anxiety, social dysfunction, inability to grasp subtext and sarcasm, obsessive tendencies and avoidance of physical contact.

His character has most definitely changed viewers perceptions and interpretation of the autism spectrum.

Autism awareness, TV shows, charities, campaigners, advocates, and so on are alerting and familiarising the public on the subject of autism. However, we still seem to experience this huge gap and misunderstanding of autistic differences as a spectrum.

One of the most common examples of child autistic behaviour that is publicised within society is that if you see a child in a supermarket kicking and screaming on the floor, that child is most likely autistic. Because of this, it has now become one of the many typical stereotypes of an autistic child. While I agree, this example shows how a child responds to an unpredictable environment (loud noises, bright lights, over- crowded, busy places). There is also an alternative explanation. The child could simply be kicking and screaming on the floor because they wanted a toy, and the parent said *no*. In reality, there is a huge difference between an autistic child and a naughty child. The reason behind the behaviour is what makes them different.

When I think of behaviour regarding autism, I view behaviour as a form of communication:

- How is the child reacting to their environment?
- How does the child interact with people?
- Does the child respond appropriately or inappropriately?
- Is the child understanding and processing the situation?

- Does the parent understand the child's specific communication style?
- Is the child in a state of distress?

The way a child reacts, responds, and interacts with people and their environment, determines how they will behave concerning language and communication.

If an autistic child doesn't know how to communicate effectively or isn't understood, then it's inevitable they will use behavioural techniques to connect. Why? Because they haven't been taught an alternative way.

The aspects of behaviour the parent needs to think about are:

- What is the child trying to communicate? Tired, overstimulated, confused, stressed, hungry, anxious, overwhelmed.
- Is the child having difficulties and needs guidance? Doesn't know what to do or how to ask for help?
- Is the child experiencing negative input? Sensory overload, social exhaustion, being bullied, struggling to 'fit in', routines disrupted, too many changes?
- Are the child's needs met? Sufficient support in school/at home.
- Are there any triggers/stressors?
- Is there a repetitive pattern?
- What eases or makes the behaviour worse?
- Is the child behaving to create a reaction from the parent? Requires mental, physical or emotional stimulation?

- Does the child recognise their behaviour? Do they have differences in how they communicate their needs?

Being mindful of autistic behaviours.

With autistic children, there generally is an underlying motive that provokes the behaviour. However, I think it's also important to remember that children will have times when they want to push boundaries and test your patience; it's part of their development and learning methods. Just like some children will naturally have a mischievous personality or an abrupt, blunt temperament. It is the person who spends the most time with the child that will truly experience and learn about all the different aspects of the child's behaviour and the reasons why they occur.

When redirecting and addressing certain behaviours, it's important to remember what non-autistic people consider 'the correct way to behave' is not necessarily going to be the 'correct behaviour' of an autistic child. For example, an autistic child may like to shout when speaking, and talk 'at' you, instead of talking 'with you', they may constantly interrupt and talk over you. Socially, this can be viewed as rude behaviour. The way the autistic child is talking is their typical social behaviour, so they don't know how to use any other way of socialising or the typical social norms. If an autistic child isn't shown the non-autistic way, they may not naturally pick up on their social differences.

When addressing a behaviour, it is important to:

Explain the behaviour to the child. Break it down into segments, try to discuss it from both an autistic and a non-autistic perspective then they can recognise their differences. Give details of what is acceptable and unacceptable, typical behaviour, and so on. Explain how you would like them to respond next time or how to use the typically expected behaviour around family or at school. Explain why and what the consequences are.

Do not let your child's autistic diagnosis be an excuse for naughty behaviour. They still need to learn discipline when they have intentionally misbehaved

Autistic children will need alternative discipline methods, e.g., such as talking calmly, giving them time to process what they have misunderstood, done differently, disobeyed, and so on. In addition, you may need to provide visual aids (written social stories, picture cards, YouTube videos, Google Images) or give literal examples of things that have happened in the past so they can relate to what you are trying to communicate.

Recognise if your child has understood your explanation regarding their behaviour. Also, ensure you validate them and let them give their input on why they have behaved in that particular way.

Support them when rectifying reoccurring hostile behaviours. For example, give the child a calm, safe, quiet, comfortable space to go to, so they can desensitise and calm down, enabling them to respond in a coherent manner. Maybe write a list of instructions together, this can be put on a wall or in a place that is easily accessible, so the child can follow them when they need to.

Teach them the difference between needs and wants, boundaries and self-control. Their thought process may not naturally differentiate between these behaviours, therefore, will impact their actions, choices and the way they conduct themselves in the future.

Recognise if your child picks up on other people's changes in behaviour; happy to sad, fun to annoying. This will impact how your child responds and reacts to people.

Re-enforce rules, boundaries, acceptable and unaccepta-ble behaviours—consistency is very important.

Meltdowns and tantrums.

It is very common for autistic people to experience autistic meltdowns. A meltdown occurs when a person becomes completely overwhelmed and loses total self-control of their emotions and actions. Meltdowns are often mistaken for tantrums. The differences are:

A tantrum is paraded verbally and/or physically by the child, with the main intention of gaining a want, a need or a specific goal. The child will check to ensure their behaviour has your attention, wilfully acting out in front of an audience. Once they have got what they need/want the behaviour halts.

A meltdown is provoked by a response to an over-stimulated environment or feelings of anxiety, overwhelmed or scared. The child isn't looking to gain anything or any specific goals, nor do they require maintaining your attention for a response. The meltdown will stop once they have taken control of their environment and calmed down; by using a coping strategy, stim, or assistance from a helper.

An autistic meltdown can last for minutes, hours or even days. It can be particularly difficult to differentiate between a tantrum and a meltdown in children because both can exhibit behaviours such as shouting, screaming, swearing, biting, throwing things and hitting.

An autistic meltdown, just like a tantrum, can also result from a child not getting their own way or they are told to do something they don't like. Their response is usually verbalised in a boisterous over-the-top manner. This is where the confusion lies for most parents. With the autistic meltdown, the behaviour could be because the child is feeling uncomfortable with a situation, misunderstanding what they are meant to do, or not understanding why they can't have something. Or it could be because the autistic child started with a tantrum that has got out of control then triggered an autistic meltdown.

In life, whether a person behaves good, bad, appropriately, or inappropriately, either way, there will no doubt be times when the person is subjected to other people's judgements and unwanted comments. It's the autistic persons' awareness of their own characteristics and an understanding of their behaviours that will help them learn how to respond, react, and cope in these unpredictable situations.

My son is a calm introverted child. Who rarely behaves inappropriately or misbehaves. He loves rules and structure (it also helps that I understand how to respond to his needs). It's daily tasks such as getting ready for school or tidying up his things, that he will meltdown over.

One time, when asking him to tidy up, I knew it wasn't a tantrum because he literally went from totally fine to full-on throwing himself around. In this state of mind, I can't talk to him. He shuts down, and there's no response. It's like he has to go through this outraged emotion—get it all out, then when that's done, he'll calm instantly and say, "Sorry, Mum." As if nothing ever happened.

I realised the stressor was because he didn't understand how to independently tidy his things up and put them back into the correct places. The whole process of tidying and the instructions given by me had completely over-whelmed him. Even though he knew he had a box for his cars and a shelf for his books, he still needed me to break down the process of putting things back. So, we sat to-gether and made a large list (poster) with a photo at the side of each instruction showing where the toys go. This went on his bedroom wall. So, all he had to do was look at, 'Number 1: Put books on the shelf.' A photo was next to it showing the books on the shelf. 'Number 2: Put dirty clothes in the wash basket.' A photo of the wash basket was also placed beside the instruction, and so on. To this day, I still sit with him and go through the list, guiding him through the instructions. I don't tidy his things; I want him to learn this responsibility, and at the same time, look after his toys and own space.

When my son was younger, I used completely different strategies when trying to help reduce and control his meltdowns. We would turn things into a game, e.g., who could put the most cars in the box, who could find the most red or blue Lego bricks. I've had to learn what works best for him. Diverting his attention from the situation and putting it into a much easier-to-comprehend task has helped me include my son and teach him to adapt.

I'll never forget one particular meltdown that my son experienced when he was three years old. As a family, we had gone to a train museum for the day (he loved Thomas the Tank Engine as a little boy). The issue was, we had to go on a bus to get to the museum. I'd never taken him on a bus before, so I wasn't sure how he would react. When the bus pulled up, he seemed fine until we sat down, and the bus pulled away. Then, the noise, the motion, the lights, the people, everything triggered him. He was in a full-blown meltdown, kicking and screaming. I had every single person staring at me. I could feel their eyes on me as if to say, *'look at that naughty child, can't she deal with him?'* All I wanted to do was help my child and calm him.

I sat him on my knee, put his face into my chest to block out all the lights, wrapped my arm around his head so I could cover his ears, and rocked him back and forth to balance the unpredictable motion, and blew constant shushing sounds into his ears (this sound always calmed him). As he calmed, I looked around at the faces staring at me. I just wanted to scream, *'he's a child! An autistic child! Stop with your judgemental stares!'* But no, they viewed me as that useless mother with the annoying naughty child.

For me, when I experience a meltdown, I go one of two ways. I either shut down or go into a full-blown explosive out-of-control distressed state. When I shut down, I have to lie down or sit, I can't have any noise at all, or it will trigger me a thousand times more, that means nobody talks to me, no background noise, nothing. In my head, I have a million scenarios racing through my mind, trying to make sense of my feelings and why my anxiety is through the roof. I have all these discussions with myself:

Did I do this, should I have done that, why did that happen, what did I say, did I say it right, what did I forget, what was I supposed to do?

It's like my brain doesn't know how to function and is about to explode.

When I experience meltdowns that make me react in an out of control emotional state, mine are usually caused by social exhaustion or auditory (sensory) overload. I struggle to talk and rarely make sense. I forget things and talk frantically. I pace constantly, I'm totally irrational in my decisions, and the way I talk, I will flip from emotion to emotion. I have to shut myself off from everything and be on my own so that I can calm my mind and body.

Luckily, I have learned what a meltdown feels like *for me* and understand how to calm myself. But, even though I have this awareness, I still really don't like it when I am like this and the impact a meltdown has on me. It's like the meltdown creates an aftermath of emotions that impacts me for days afterwards.

Meltdowns can also be very physical. Many children will throw themselves on the floor, head-banging, kicking, screaming and lashing out. They may physically hit or verbally attack you. When a child is young, they can be managed and supported, but it is not so easy when the child hits an age where they have brutal strength and vicious verbal outbursts. You can find yourself in a predicament where you honestly don't know how to support them.

This is a complex issue and will be entirely subjective to the child based on their stressors and triggers, environment, support, communication abilities, etc.

For safety reasons, coping strategies need to be put in place. How you do this will involve many factors, for instance:

- Learning how to calm the child/teaching the child how to calm themselves. This requires quiet calm voices. Don't throw more negative energy into an already destructive situation; it will only cause additional stressors and could possibly trigger them to fall into a self-destructive state of mind.
- How you react will ultimately impact how they respond. Try to reduce your verbal communication,

don't overcrowd them. Talking at them whilst in a
state of distress can potentially affect their
emotional responses and reactions.
- Be their safety net. Maybe they just need you to
leave them to calm down on their own, in their own
quiet space. Or, they may need you to hold them,
rock them, stroke their head—whatever it may be,
you need to observe their reaction and response and
detect what works best for them.

There will be times when I accidentally trigger my child.
For example, I sometimes forget to prepare my child with
verbal instructions when I need him to do something, i.e.,
before bedtime, I have to do a countdown, telling him
fifteen minutes left, then remind him at ten minutes, then
one minute. This helps him refocus his attention on
what's happening next and allows him to prepare himself
for the routine tasks. If I forget to do this, it will trigger a
meltdown. In the past, he has hit me, lashed out, verbally
attacked me, thrown himself off the sofa, basically, just
completely flipped into an outraged uncontrollable state
of emotion.

When learning how to help my son control this type
of emotional response, the first thing I do is say, "I am
sorry. It's my fault. I forgot to give you a count-down
time." Taking the pressure off him, and taking
responsibility for not recognising his needs by
acknowledging that I am the one that has triggered him,
helps him calm. He then understands why he has been
triggered, which ultimately softens the response. I then
have to start the process again, explaining it is bedtime,
saying fifteen minutes, ten minutes, and so forth.

Other situations when we have had to learn how to control his meltdowns have been regarding his computer games. My son loves to play Minecraft and Planet Coaster. I put restrictions on the time period that he spends on these games. He doesn't have his own computer; it's the *family's computer*. It is placed in the living room, so he knows he can't spend all day on it. It has to be shared (I think if he had his own computer at this age, it would create additional stressors). I have to give him a visual timer (looking at the clock, when the big hand hits six, you are to come off) and count down—ten minutes left, five minutes left, one minute left. Then he will come off without a fuss. If I don't do this, he will meltdown.

Before he goes on the computer, I lay down the rules. I tell him, "No getting angry. If a game triggers you, you come off." I want him to learn to recognise his emotions and when things are impacting him negatively. This usually prevents aggression, and he will verbalise when he is angry with the game instead of lashing out.

I won't buy him his own computer until I think he is mature enough to implement self-control, and as the parent, I will control this aspect until he can learn. This has helped create balance, and at the same time, he is learning how to conduct himself appropriately through playing and doing what he enjoys.

There have been times when I have told my son off for misbehaving, and it has triggered a meltdown (not a tantrum). Again, I have to figure out what is causing this emotional response. I have to calm him, then ask, "Do you understand why I have told you off? What have you done that has made me feel angry?" Because he doesn't automatically recognise when he has upset me and why I have responded in a stern manner. Or he may do something that he doesn't realise is naughty, therefore not recognise why he is being disciplined. I find when I ask him, "Why have I told you off?" he generally says, "I don't know," or he will give a reason that is entirely irrelevant to what has just happened because he has read the situation completely wrong.

Again, this is why I say break things down, so you can understand the emotional response. If he misunderstands the situation, I have to explain in great detail what he has done that is wrong, why it is wrong, and how he should have behaved differently/appropriately. Therefore, next time, he will know how to conduct himself accordingly and understand why I reacted.

Through this, my son is now starting to vocalise when he misunderstands situations before they escalate into bigger problems. Again, no two situations are ever the same. What it comes down to is knowing how to apply basic strategies so you can understand how to help your child communicate and recognise the causal factors of their emotional response, and what and why they are using particular behaviours to respond, react and communicate.

Chapter 10

Helping Your Child to Thrive

As parents, it's natural to want to see your child happy and enjoying everything that life offers. The love and laughter a child brings to a family are wonderful. The fun and enjoyment pave the way for feelings of joy and happy memories. But, along the way, life can come with many challenges and can make parenting very difficult at times—creating not so much happy memories but worry and strife.

When parenting an autistic child, one thing you'll no doubt learn is you have many hidden aspects to yourself and your personality—more than you could have ever realised. We find these hidden qualities because we have times where we're made to step out of our comfort zones and push ourselves to be the person our child needs us to be.

Previously I have discussed how it's important to acknowledge how other people may impact you and your child. To help your child thrive, it is also important to recognise your impact on your child and how you react and respond as a parent.

A child (autistic or not) will respond to your energy, demeanour, manners, personality traits, and so on. The personality traits will have a huge impact on how your child responds to you, e.g., are you patient, erratic, calm, lively, quiet, loud, organised, forgetful, laid back, strict?

Do you have patterns of unpredictable behaviour? If so, do you recognise them, do they conflict with your child's behaviours? Do you trigger your child? Do you have to adjust your routine to fit theirs, or do you make them adapt to yours? Maybe there is no routine? Are you organised or sporadic? Do you have good time management, or are you all over the place? Are you a good listener? Or do you like people to listen to you?

There are so many contributing aspects to our own character that will undoubtedly influence the connection between you and your child.

It could also help if you acknowledge how your child makes you feel. Your child may cause you to have specific triggers that stress you. For example, a child constantly talking, asking the same questions over and over could become irritating.

If your child triggers you, how do you react and respond? In a hasty manner, or are you calm? Do you explain why you're annoyed?

You may find you and your child are complete opposites

and experience a clash of personalities. You may have to adapt many aspects of yourself to help create shared interests and commonalities. Or you and your child may share many similarities and interests. Either way, this is something you will recognise personally and for you to explore as your child gets older.

The way we present ourselves and utilise our parenting skills will naturally impact the child and determine how they fit into the family unit. As adults, we rarely reflect on ourselves, looking at our own behaviour and how we respond and react to situations, forgetting that how we present ourselves can impact our child in both positive and negative ways.

Ultimately, the way you parent your child will impact them as a person as they grow into adulthood.

It's not only the parents that will help the child thrive, but the environment we bring them up in, the guidance we provide, the experiences they will have, and the life skills we teach, for instance:

- How to make a basic snack, drink or meal.
- How to save, budget and manage money.
- How to be responsible, e.g., prepare their own school bag.
- Time management (getting to school on time, allowing time for school homework).
- Decision making (looking at advantages and disadvantages before making a decision).
- Basic first aid (cleaning a cut or a scratch and putting on a plaster/band-aid).

- How to tidy, clean and do basic household chores.
- The importance of health (eating fruit and vegetables, drinking enough water).
- How to maintain basic hygiene (cleaning teeth, showering).
- How to use basic etiquette and manners (when buying in a shop or eating in a restaurant).

Parents also have the responsibility of teaching their child about the society we live in, for example, explaining the reasons behind rules and laws, especially when out in public, school, etc. They need to know why society requires you to abide by the rules and the consequences of breaking them.

A child also needs teaching self-awareness of their own behaviours. For example, do they have anxiety, are they triggered easily, do they respond appropriately?

Children with autism don't tend to naturally learn how to regulate their behaviour and emotions, unlike non-autistic children. This means they don't always recognise when and how to control disordered outbursts of violence towards others and their possessions. It is common for some autistic children to use anger and aggression when they're triggered or cannot communicate effectively or when they simply can't get their own way.

If you are a parent of a child that's prone to smashing things, you are no doubt going to have to remove anything that can potentially be harmful to them or yourself. Especially if the child has no self-control and is unpredictable in their behaviour. I hear all too often that a child has put their fist through a wall or a door. Some have smashed their television, iPad, or mobile phone. Whether the damage is intentional or unintentional, the child needs to understand if any items or situations will put them in danger, then the items (or the child) will need to be removed for their own safety. It's imperative that a child recognises the impact they have on others due to their own actions.

It can also be very costly to just keep replacing things without correcting and addressing the behaviour or putting a coping strategy in place. Yes, you can buy screen protectors for televisions, mobile phones and iPads, they come in handy in these situations, but they don't guarantee your child isn't going to be harmed when they are in a state of rage and taking their anger out on these items. A child will no doubt fail to thrive if repetitive situations like this are not addressed.

Always remember safety first. If you need to take drastic measures and remove items from their bedroom, just for your peace of mind, so you know they aren't causing damage or harming themselves, then the minimalistic approach is what you need to do. You can still give them a television, iPad, etc, but only put items in a room where you know you can control the situation if it gets out of hand. Don't feel guilty for removing things and putting yours and their safety first.

Initially, removing things can trigger them even more and create additional aggression. Preparations will most definitely need to be put in place but remember you are the parent; it's your house, your rules.

If the aggression isn't a behaviour and is centred around a meltdown, in that case, it's important to let them focus their aggression via a controlled outlet such as:

Stress balls, giving them a football to go kick at a wall/net, provide them with a trampoline to throw themselves on, or put a pile of cushions on the floor for them to fling themselves into and punch if they need to.

I know many parents who have bought a punch bag for their child to relieve their aggression. Of course, I'm not suggesting you buy a punch bag, but it just shows there are many alternative ways to use when helping a child redirect their anger.

Try to recognise when your child has been triggered, so you can put in the appropriate measures and redirect them straight away. With some children, you won't know when a meltdown is coming on; it's in these unpredictable situations where you just have to make sure the child is out of harm and let them know you are there to support them if need be.

When the child is in a calm state, sit down with them and ask how you can help them when they are in a distressed state of mind. Can they tell you what emotion they are experiencing? Is it the physical stimulation that helps them to get out their frustration or calm down?

With autism, the tricky part is trying to work out, is it a meltdown, or is it child/teenage behaviour (pushing boundaries)? If the child is behaving aggressively because they want a reaction from you, or because you are enforcing rules or saying no to a situation, then you know the child is controlling the issue, and they're using volatile behaviour to get what they want. How you respond and manage the problem will inevitably impact their reaction. If a parent doesn't address, redirect, or control the child's behaviour, then the child will no doubt keep on acting that way because the situation is staying the same, and they don't know any other way.

Alternatively, try teaching the child how to behave appropriately to get what they want, reinforce these strategies. Always explain and reiterate the reasons why you have put in restrictions or provided consequences.

Ultimately, a child will have to learn coping strategies and conduct themselves appropriately towards other people throughout their lives. These are fundamental qualities that we require as an adult to maintain employment, attain relationships, and so on. Suppose the child continues with inappropriate behaviours throughout childhood and into adulthood without recognising how to calm or control themselves. It will no doubt have a detrimental effect on their mental health and well-being. These behaviours can become ingrained habits, therefore, become very difficult to adjust if needed.

It's common to hear parents of autistic children being called 'Warrior Mums/Dads' or parents may say, "God only picks the best people to parent an autistic child." This view is because parents of autistic children know in order to help their child thrive and function adequately in the world, there will generally be hundreds of adjustments needed within the family unit. Because parenting an autistic child is entirely different from parenting a non-autistic child.

Chapter 11

Emotional Connections and

Self-Confidence

It is common for autistic children and adults to suffer terribly with poor self-esteem and low self-confidence. This can additionally lead to self-destructive behaviours and cause them to withdraw from taking part with others. This can be because of many factors, such as:

- Feeling like they don't fit in.
- Think they appear weird or different to others.
- Don't feel compatible or like they connect with people on a similar level.
- Struggle to express themselves effectively.
- They're misunderstood.
- Don't know how to integrate with others to form friendships.

It can also be difficult for some autistic people to accept praise or compliments—simply because they can't see how others view them. For example, somebody could say to an autistic child, *'you are amazing'* a hundred times or more, but they will still find a way to pick at themselves and find faults because of low self-esteem.

Self-love and acceptance of who they are can also be difficult for them. No matter how hard they may try, they can still feel invalidated. This is another reason why we see so many children falling into a state of self-destruction. For some, it can be because the society and environment that they live in feel very alien to them.

The main causes of my low confidence and poor self-esteem connect to communication. Our day-to-day living inevitably requires us to converse with others — I struggle when talking to people I don't know very well. I find it difficult to just go up to somebody and strike up a random conversation, even when there is a given purpose, or if they talk to me first, I will still find it problematic. Yes, it makes it easier when people lead the conversation, but I still experience strong feelings of social anxiety. This impacts my confidence immensely and prevents me from seeking friendships, certain jobs, joining social groups or a gym.

Keeping myself to myself is easier than the stress of maintaining social connections, such as friendships. My friends that I socialise with are generally those that I have known for years. This is how I protect myself from putting myself in situations where I know I am setting myself up to fail. I often question, if I could communicate like a non-autistic person would my confidence grow? But, at almost forty years of age, I know the way I communicate will not change. But that doesn't mean to say I don't push myself beyond my boundaries. On the contrary, I've learnt how to deal with it so I can get past the self-destructive behaviours. I don't beat myself up about it anymore. I just accept it's the way I am and the way I will always be.

Again, this results from self-awareness and an understanding of my difficulties. Prior to this knowledge, I put way too much pressure on myself to make friends. This resulted in making some poor choices regarding friendships and befriending people who caused me great stress. As a result, I am now more careful about who I let into my social circle.

Connecting with your child on an emotional level.

I have had many years of learning how I connect with others on a personal level and what emotions it evokes from these connections. As parents, when we connect with children on an emotional level, it's not just verbal but also physical. This is because, from the moment a child comes into the world, the baby is wrapped up tight in a parent's arms, and we instantly feel the love. That physical and emotional connection typically continues throughout that first year via non-verbal communication; due to the child's absent language skills. Then, when a child reaches nursery/school age, we offer shared verbal and physical affection to reassure a child and provide comfort.

Think about how your child has connected and responded to your physical and emotional affection throughout their life. How does your child interact now?

Does your child like cuddles and kisses? Or do they prefer a high five or a fist pump? Or maybe they don't like any physical contact at all, and would prefer a thumbs up, or an okay sign? These positive forms of expressive communication help form emotional bonds and provide a path that helps us connect with our child one-to-one. The loving action prompts a response. The child may give constant cuddles back, or they may simply just nod their head as a polite yes, or reciprocate a thumbs up. Either way, the point is, your child will have years practising and learning how to receive and reciprocate emotional connections.

Recognising how your child prefers to engage on an emotional level will help you develop further personal connections. You can use this contact to form bonds and let them acknowledge when you appreciate their good behaviour. So, when your child is naughty and doesn't get a positive physical-emotional response from you, they will see the obvious difference in your demeanour.

This can be useful for children that don't pick up on social cues such as body language and facial expressions. The action can be physical rather than visual. For example, if the child doesn't respond with a smile or use facial expressions, a simple high five will let you know they have acknowledged when they have done good or let you know they are happy.

When autistic children are emotionally distressed, they can switch off and block out people, voices, shouting, familiar and unfamiliar sounds, and refrain from verbal communication. This is another time when your child can use physical gestures to respond. They don't necessarily need to use reciprocal language, just a gentle hug or a thumbs up can be used to show emotional support.

Many parents tend to use material items or buy things such as sweets and toys to engage the child emotionally. It's the reward that creates the emotional response. The child is shown sentiment with a physical item rather than a verbal or physical gesture. This is fine, but when buying or giving material items or money becomes a habit, it forms an emotional response, sort of like a contract. Meaning you are creating an agreement that it is normal practice to just give, give, give, and make it so it's okay to bargain with the child when you want them to behave or do things you require of them. This emotional response is evoked because that's how the parent has taught the child to emotionally connect, rather than, creating a natural emotional bond with no conditions.

In my opinion, a good person to use as an example (regarding emotional connection) that most people of my generation have heard of in the UK is Katie Price (model and business woman) and her son Harvey.

Katie has been in the public eye for the last twenty-five years or so, and is very public about her life and the journey she has been on with Harvey. Harvey has many disabilities, including autism. He needs 24-hour support because of his high level of needs. In addition, Harvey is intellectually disabled with learning difficulties. But through all this, Katie has still found a way to engage him emotionally and connect with him.

This has no doubt impacted Harvey's quality of life in the utmost positive way. For those of you that do know of Katie (whether you like or dislike her), in my opinion she is getting everything right with Harvey. I watch her connect with him on the sincerest emotional level (one-to-one), and the bond they have is beautiful. She engages him via his special interests, understands his sensory difficulties, understands what triggers him and most of all, connects with Harvey on his level.

I am sure there are many times when Harvey has horrendous meltdowns and mischievous moments like other autistic children. But what we see with Katie is the coping strategies and emotional connection that she has worked extremely hard on to develop. Yes, there's no denying she is in a privileged position being in the public eye. And may have had additional support throughout the years (nannies, etc), which would have helped tremendously. But in truth, all the money in the world could not buy an emotional bond like Katie has with Harvey. She has done that herself.

In the past, Katie has received a torrent of abuse online regarding Harvey's disabilities. She has spoken openly about this on television and in the media. I can't even begin to imagine how this must have impacted her mental health. Like any child, all parents want to do is protect their children from hurt. In Katie's circumstances, she's had no choice but to go above and beyond to shield Harvey from abuse.

As parents of autistic children, people think we can just put on this imaginary metal armour and fight every battle. When in reality, a lot of parents just hide behind that armour. The attacking happens on the inside, in our mind, that's where the real battles are.

So, to reiterate, parents really need to be mindful of how they emotionally connect with their child—we are the ones who influence and support them.

Recognise how they reach out to you emotionally, so you can help develop harmonious connections.

Low self-confidence.

Many factors can impact low self-confidence. Personally, I think fear is one of the biggest influences. Yes, we all experience fear at some stages in life, but with autism, fear can be a constant battle, more so with fears such as:

- Failing and doing things wrong.
- Being judged and misunderstood.
- Feeling out of control.
- Being subjected to unpredictable environments and surroundings.
- Unable to control other people's actions and reactions.

- Unable to communicate effectively.
- Loud noises (vacuum cleaner, dogs barking, leaf blower, lawn mower, hair dryer, washing machine).
- Being in a room by yourself (at night/in the dark).
- Insects (butterflies, spiders, wasps).
- Going through the carwash (with parents).
- Strangers/crowds.
- Using public toilets (hand dryers' noise, toilets flushing noise, germs -touching door handles, taps).
- Haircuts, toes/fingernails being clipped.
- Elevators, escalators, electronic sliding/rotating doors.
- Storms, thunder and lightning, fireworks.

Many things can create fear for a child. Does your child have any fears? Maybe they only have one or multiple fears?

It can be very difficult for parents to enter their child's mind and identify what is causing the distressing emotions and feelings, which could negatively affect their confidence. It can be just as complicated when trying to pinpoint how to help.

If a child is already in a state of distress, it may be difficult for them to open up and express what is affecting them. It can be a slow process of breaking down the areas that cause the most fear. Helping the child take control and understand how to push past or surrender to the fear may help them and provide an outlet to see they can achieve things if they put their mind to it and work past it.

For an autistic person to push themselves beyond their

boundaries is no easy feat; respect the fact this will take great effort. It might not come naturally for the child to be fearless, but, like most difficulties, you will need to recognise the child's limitations and what impact the fear is having on the child. Is it creating additional behaviours? Can you push them to break the barriers down, or does it make them worse? Do they need counselling or assisted support? Is there a root cause to the fear that can be addressed? Is the child overanalysing everything? Do they express their worries or internalise them?

Depending on your child's age and level of understanding, can you take the lead and show your child how to get past the fear to help build confidence?

If they are verbal, can you use social stories, write or draw the situation on paper, let the child talk about it, see what is causing them to feel so afraid, and see if there is anything you can do to help them.

Take small steps, one day at a time and if the child refuses to participate, acknowledge that the child is clearly in a state of distress. Goading a child or forcing them into doing something they clearly find extremely difficult will only make them worse.

My son has a huge fear of going on theme park rides. This is something I also struggle with; I can't tolerate the anticipation that builds up before the ride starts. I also don't like the speed or the impact the force of the ride has on my body. The adrenaline rush has the opposite effect on me. Where some people might have what's called an adrenaline high, I don't; I feel a horrendous sense of anxiety. I guess this is my difference and how I process the sensations differently.

We recently had a funfair come to our local town. My daughter loves the fairground rides, as does my husband, so we went along. As soon as I asked my son, "Do you want to go on a ride?" I could see the question petrified him. Like me, he does not get any joy from it at all. The noise, the lights, everything becomes overwhelming for him, so I am very mindful of how much he can tolerate. We tend to just play the games such as hook a duck, throwing bean bags at stacked cans and shooting the targets.

Just as we were about to leave, my son decided he wanted to go on a ride. Straight away, I looked for the slowest, calmest ride that I could go on with him. He then changed his mind. "No, I can't do it!" I could see he really wanted to have a go like the other children, but it all became too much for him to control.

I then said, "I will ask the lady to stop the ride if you want to get off at any time. How about that?" He seemed okay with that. I explained the situation to the lady controlling the ride. She was more than happy to accommodate our needs. We chose a train ride with carriages; it went around in a continuous slow circle. The train was big enough for my daughter to sit in the front and my son and me in the back.

Waiting for the ride to start, I could see the anticipation in him building up just like mine does. I refocused his attention. "Look towards Dad, smile at the camera." Then we were off. He squeezed my hand and instantly started worrying, mumbling and chattering at me in distress. Suddenly, he realised he was fine; he could tolerate it as it wasn't as fast as he'd anticipated. I saw his little face light up. I just felt so happy for him and proud that he had pushed through his fear. It was a huge step for him.

Chapter 12

What Does Autism Teach Us?

When I reflect on all the things that I've learnt from parenting an autistic child, studying autism at university, and simply by just being autistic myself, it brings a rollercoaster of emotions. Especially when I think back to before my son was born. I couldn't have ever imagined that I would have been on this unique, eye-opening journey, one that has taught me countless life lessons that are beyond thinkable.

I have learnt new aspects, including:

- All the different dynamics involved with language and communication, e.g. the way a child learns to speak, how they process and implement language, which aspects of language take longer to develop, what a child may process differently or misunderstand.
- The complex depths surrounding sensory difficulties and what they entail.

- How meltdowns can be triggered completely different one day to the next. How to prevent meltdowns, and how they impact the child.
- I've learnt we all have huge varying levels of abilities and limitations and have specific boundaries that control how far we will push ourselves.
- How to be mindful of healthy mental health and a person's well-being.

Remember, as a parent, it will take you time to learn all the intricacies of your child's specific autism characteristics; it will not happen overnight. You will encounter your own personal journey.

Even though I am autistic and I have had to learn about myself and what being autistic means for me, I am thankful that I have also had the gratification of learning about my son and his autism journey—learning how he interacts and connects with the world.

He has taught me a great deal about things, such as:

- Patience.
- How to listen when he couldn't even talk.
- How to try, try, and try again, and never give up.
- To never judge a situation or anyone before you clearly understand them.
- To not place expectations on anything.
- To appreciate the now.
- To celebrate the smallest achievements in life, they all count.
- To not be too hard on myself, I am doing my best.

- To not care what other people think of me or our situation.
- To remember, not everyone will understand the complexities of autism.
- To ignore negativity from other people, instead, realise it does not serve me.
- To recognise my child is giving me experiences that are helping me grow as a person.
- That love is unconditional.
- And most importantly, to accept my child no matter how different he may appear to other children, he is perfectly autistic to me.

Love truly does change everything. The love for our children drives us to constantly fight their battles and want to give them everything they need to live the best life possible.

I have also learnt that we are all different, we all have our own struggles, and we all need to feel connected. Whether that is through families, lovers, friends, children, animals, music, hobbies, travelling to different countries, special interests, whatever it may be. We somehow want to experience some sort of connection to feel happy and fulfilled. Our differences are what influence and affect how we reach and accomplish those connections.

Along the way, don't forget to think about yourself, and how you are holding up and dealing with all the differences that your child may bring. You are allowed to feel frustrated and stressed at times. I don't think you'll find many parents that don't have times like that.

Don't feel ashamed for having days when you wish you could magically make autism and everything that autism brings to your family just disappear in an instant, or wishing you could understand everything about your child's needs.

You may have phases where you're exhausted and feel alone. Just remember, you are doing your best for your child. If you need help, don't be afraid to speak out. We can't understand absolutely everything there is to know about our children, there will be times when you need to say, "Somebody, anybody, I need help please!" And this is totally acceptable.

If you have more than one child, don't feel guilty about treating them differently from each other. One child may have your undivided attention, which may impact another child, because each child may have different needs. It is a fine balancing act that, at times, can feel out of control. Just recognise, each child is different, and you are doing your best.

Remember to take time out for yourself. Explain to family or friends you need 'me time' for your own sanity. You are not a machine, you are human, and we all need to be mindful of our own needs no matter how much somebody else may depend on you. Even if it's just watching a movie on your own, or going for a quiet walk, give yourself time to clear your mind of any stresses or worries. You need healthy mental health just as much as your child does.

And remember, autism is your child's normal.

Perfectly autistic

...in every single way.

Thanks for reading!

Amazon reviews are extremely helpful for authors.

Please add a review on Amazon and let me know what you thought. Thank you.

Emma xxx

Helping You to Identify and Understand Autism Masking

Emma shares her unique insights and personal experiences describing what autism masking is. She also reveals the intriguing motives for the use of this behaviour. Explaining how autistic people do this and why, and to what extent the mask is relied upon, as well as uncovering fascinating details concerning the after-effects and the long-term impact of autism masking.

Autistic Christmas
How to Prepare for an Autism Friendly Christmas

Being a parent to a child on the autism spectrum can be challenging at the best of times, but when you add a very busy season to the mix, full of confusing Christmas traditions, visual changes, social events, and disruptions to routine, it can become even trickier. Whether you're making plans to visit family and friends, or having a quiet, peaceful Christmas at home, there will be many preparations that need to be considered.

Adele Fox Series Book One

Making Sense of Love

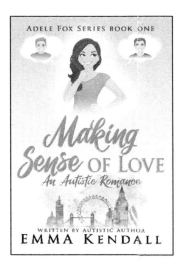

Autistic… single… and not quite sure how to mingle.

As Adele Fox approaches thirty—being single is her normal. Would she like a boyfriend? Yes. Does she know how to date? Not exactly.

Making small talk, flirting, reading body language, understanding jokes and sarcasm—sounds easy right? That is unless you have a communication difference.

When a chance encounter brings Adele together with a charming travel agent, she finds herself being whisked away for a romantic Valentine's weekend. Little does she know, her world is about to be turned upside down.

Adele Fox Series Book Two

A Different Kind of Love

Autistic… In love… And ready to start the next chapter in her life.
Not only has Adele Fox found her dream man, she's also found a new home, a new job and a host of other dilemmas to go with it.

When Adele's differences complicate matters with her new work colleagues, she takes a trip back to her familiar life in London, when an old flame from her past unexpectedly returns, throwing her life into a spin, which leads her to question:

Was the huge life change worth it? Was it the right decision? Is she capable of being loved?

Adele Fox Series Book Three

Memories Full of Love

Autistic… newly married… and trying to fit into a new family.

As Adele Fox enters married life as Mrs Beeton, not only does she have to adjust to becoming a wife, she also has to form a relationship with her husband's parents.

Whilst on their honeymoon, Adele unexpectedly finds out about a Beeton family secret that has been kept hidden and buried for years.

Little does she know, what she says, and what she hides will have consequences and could ruin her marriage.

Does Adele ruin her relationship with her new family? Will she overcome and reveal her own secret?

Printed in Great Britain
by Amazon